Your Health in Your
Hands

Your Health in Your Hands

Palmistry for health and well-being

Lori Reid

JOURNEY EDITIONS

Boston • Tokyo • Singapore

To Peter West — good friend and colleague, with love and thanks

PLEASE NOTE
The author, packager and publisher cannot accept any responsibility for misadventure resulting from the practice of any of the principles and therapies set out in this book. This book is not intended for the treatment of serious health problems; please refer to a medical professional if you are in any doubt about any aspect of your condition.

First published in the United States in 2002 by Journey Editions, an imprint of Periplus Editions (HK) Ltd., with editorial offices at 153 Milk Street, Boston, Massachusetts 02109.

Library of Congress Control Number: 2002103991

ISBN: 1-58290-065-5

Distributed by

North America, Latin America & Europe	Japan & Korea	Asia Pacific
Tuttle Publishing Distribution Center Airport Industrial Park 364 Innovation Drive North Clarendon VT 05759-9436 Tel: (802) 773-8930 Tel: (800) 526-2778 Fax: (802) 773-6993	Tuttle Publishing Yaekari Building 3F 5-14-12 Ōsaki Shinagawa–ku Tokyo 141–0032 Tel: (03) 5437-0171 Fax: (03) 5437-0755	Berkeley Books Pte Ltd 130 Joo Seng Road #06-01/03 Olivinc Building Singapore 368357 Tel: (65) 6280-1330 Fax: (65) 6280-6290

First edition
07 06 05 04 03 02   10 9 8 7 6 5 4 3 2 1

AN EDDISON•SADD EDITION
Edited, designed and produced by
Eddison Sadd Editions Limited
St Chad's House, 148 King's Cross Road
London WC1X 9DH

Phototypeset in Bembo MT and News Gothic BT using QuarkXPress on Apple Macintosh
Origination by C.H. Colour Scan SDN BHD, Kuala Lumpur, Malaysia
Printed by Kyodo Printing Co., Singapore

Contents

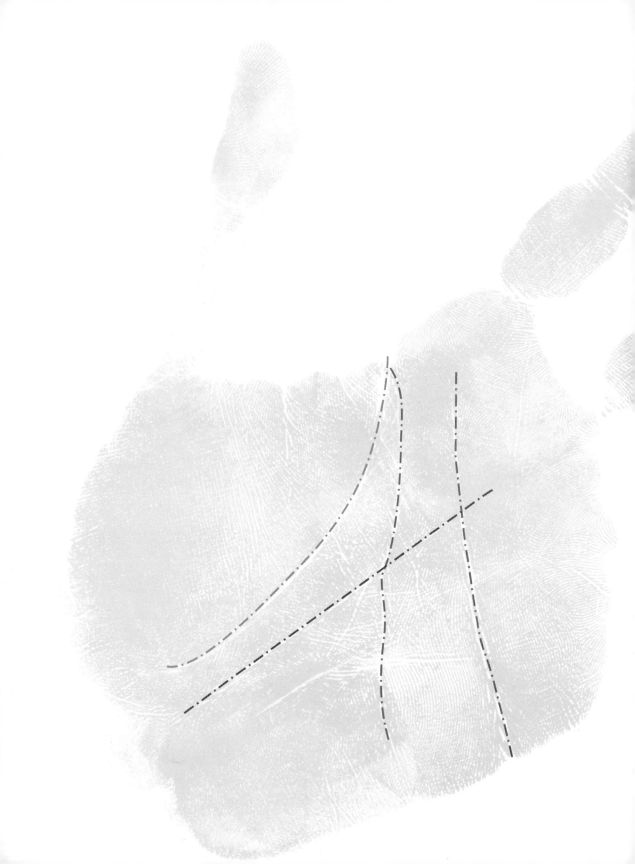

Foreword

In the same way as our genes determine the colour of our eyes, so our chromosomal blueprint lays down the shape of our hands, the patterns we recognize as fingerprints and the major lines that crisscross the palm. And we know that our personalities – also reflected in our hands – contribute a good deal to our health patterns. Our hands are living registers that record all manner of data about ourselves: how we think and behave, how we work, love and interact with others, our dreams, ambitions and conscious and subconscious motivations, our predispositions, and our psychological and physical health.

This book is about using this knowledge to promote good health. Its treatment suggestions are designed not only to address specific problems, but to promote well-being on a daily basis. You can allow your habits and lifestyle to render you vulnerable to illness, or you can choose to use your hands as a valuable diagnostic tool to pick up early clues that help you maintain your vitality and actively prevent disease from developing. In other words, you can literally take your health in your hands.

Making connections

Science has shown that people are predisposed to certain types of illness, regardless of environmental factors. And there is also little doubt that a connection exists between our hands and our health – that these predispositions can be glimpsed there. For centuries, doctors have routinely consulted the hands of their patients, not only for taking the pulse at the wrist, but also for a variety of symptoms that will back up their diagnosis of disease. For example, listless hands often accompany a lack of energy or a loss of motivation, while tremor is linked with hormonal problems, toxicity and diseases of the nervous system. However, discoloration and abnormal temperature may be caused by faulty oxygenation, problems of the cardiovascular system, fever, shock, or an imbalance of the endocrine system.

Understanding the hands

A whole host of other conditions are recognized as producing corresponding signs in the hand, and powerful indicators of

Fingertips and phalanges
Fingerprint patterns indicate specific character traits which have a direct bearing on physical and mental state of health, and lines on the phalanges (finger sections) can also have health implications.

Hand type
Your hand type reveals information on what makes you tick and indicates susceptibilities and predispositions to particular health conditions.

Palm
The lines, ridges, mounds, shape and even colour of the palms reveal a wealth of information about your physical and psychological make-up.

Major lines
The Life, Heart, Head and Fate lines. Their general appearance, condition, construction and composition provide valuable clues about physical and also mental well-being.

Mounts
The condition of the padded areas on the palm – thought to represent storehouses of vitality – highlights your salient personality and state of health.

Minor lines
Together with the major lines, these provide the missing pieces of the jigsaw to make up the whole picture.

health are found in the various markings, mounds and skin patterns in the palm, fingers and wrist (see illustrations below for a quick-reference guide). When understood, all of these messages provide valuable clues about the state of our health. They highlight our resistance and vitality, betray tell-tale hints of the build-up of toxins, reveal imbalances and everyday wear and tear and generally present a picture of our constitutional weak links and our susceptibility to disease and potential future problems.

A word of warning ...

It must be stressed that, to back up any health pointers obtained from palmistry and to get a complete health picture, you should always consult a qualified medical practitioner. Although our hands tell a very revealing story, don't make the mistake of diagnosing from the hand alone (and never from just one aspect of the hands, such as the major lines). However, knowing how to interpret the signs in your hands means that you can become aware of the subtle changes taking place in your body. And, because many of these lines and markings are in constant flux, appearing and disappearing according to your circumstances, understanding the particular configurations means that you can monitor, and intervene in, your own health – with guidance from your doctor.

Nails
The size, shape and condition of the nails, plus the appearance of the moons and colour of the nail beds, are vital in assessing state of health, and can provide early warning signs to health problems.

Fingers
The size and shape of the fingers reveal much about your character and abilities, each finger representing a different facet of life.

Thumb
The shape and length of the thumbs provide the most important indicator of psychological strengths and weaknesses.

Scientific proof

Centuries of studying and analysing hands have shown emphatically that these hand–health links exist, that signs and symptoms of our inherent predisposition to disease, as well as the possibility of future ill-health, imprint their subtle clues all over our fingers and palms. We now know that it is because our palms contain a vast concentration of nerve endings, more so than any other part of our anatomy (except the soles of our feet), that they are such superb registers of nervous responses and biochemical messages. Moreover, in recent times, scientific research has established a relationship between unusual fingerprints or skin markings and genetic or congenital abnormalities. This link is now widely recognized and may well be of great value in genetic counselling as well as an aid to general medical diagnosis.

This book traces the meaning of the hand-markings that relate to your health and well-being. It takes first a general look at the physical characteristics of your hands and introduces the features that palmistry uses to diagnose health – from hand shape, size, colour and skin texture through major palm-crossing lines, such as the Heart and Life lines, to ridges in the nails. The book then homes in further to match specific forms of markings and features with certain types of health conditions, providing a detailed resource for the palmist. Armed with this information, you can move on to the final section on positive self-help, where major health conditions and their corresponding hand-signs are summarized and expanded upon, along with a rich selection of suggested treatments, health strategies and useful 'quick fix' remedies.

Taking handprints

Taking handprints regularly reveals the really fine markings that cannot be seen by the naked eye, makes it easier to take measurements and lets you monitor changes and so take any preventative action at the earliest opportunity. Using water-soluble lino-printing inks (sold in art shops) makes the whole thing easier and cleaner – simply wash it off with soap and water. Ink-pads are useful for individual fingerprints but a solvent is needed to remove the ink. Everyday alternatives include lipstick or waxy shoe polish, although you may find that removal can be a problem. Make sure you take prints of both hands, as they must be read together for a complete picture.

What you do

1 Squeeze a small amount of ink onto your smooth surface (such as a sheet of glass or formica board) and roll out thinly with the roller (or equivalent).

2 Roll the inked roller evenly over the fingers, palm and down over the first 2–3 cm (1 in) of wrist. If using lipstick or shoe polish, apply with tissues or cotton wool.

What you need

Recommended	Substitutes
Lino printing ink	Lipstick, waxy shoe polish
A sheet of glass	Formica board, piece of kitchen foil
Printer's roller	Rolling pin or empty bottle, wrapped in clingfilm
Tissues/cotton wool	
A4 sheets of paper	
Square of foam rubber	Folded towel
Table knife	
Sharp pencil	

Photocopies

Photocopied handprints are quick and easy to take, and provide an excellent back-up to inked ones. However, they do lack the degree of detail needed to provide a sole source for analysis and they may also be distorted during the copying process, so it's important that you do just use them as a back-up.

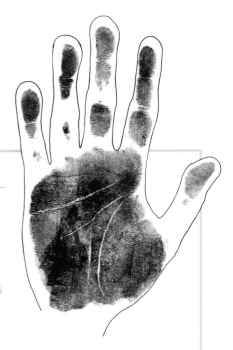

3 Put the sheet of paper onto the foam and place the inked hand on top. If you find that the centre of the palm isn't printing, then try again with the foam removed, and/or slip the knife underneath the paper and press up into the palm. Or try working the other way up, with the hand palm-side up and the paper laid on top.

4 When the hands are clean and the print dry, reposition the hand over each print and draw around the outline with the pencil. If the print is taken with the paper placed directly on the hard table top, the outline can be drawn in there and then with the inked hand still in place (but take care not to smudge your print!).

Several clear prints of each hand should be taken. Mark each with the date, owner's name, date of birth, sex and whether right- or left-handed.

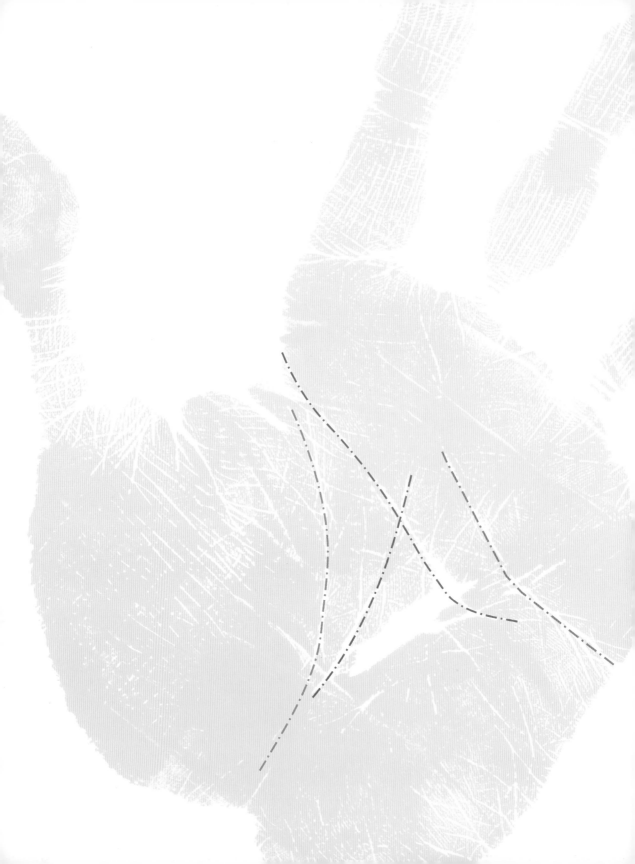

Part One

Mapping the Hands
Palmistry Basics

Your hands hold vital clues about the state of your health – the problem is knowing what signs to look for. That's where this first section of the book comes in. It introduces the fundamentals of the art of hand-reading and points out the markings that specifically relate to health. You'll find all the basic elements here: the shapes of hands and fingers, the meanings of the mounts and plains, skin texture, temperature and colour, the different fingerprints and, of course, the major and minor lines in the palm. There's also a handy step-by-step reference guide and advice on how to read your own hands and those of your friends and family. Look for the special feature pages marked with a green border, as these contain information that will not only help you to make your analysis easier and more effective, but which will also add depth to your knowledge of palmistry.

Features of the Hands

Feel and gesture

The overall feel of your hands, and the gestures that you make, give away a lot of initial information about your well-being. Taking feel first, the muscular tone should ideally be springy and elastic, neither too hard nor too soft. A resilient hand that responds like rubber to the touch denotes a vibrant constitution, with good resistance to ill-health and an ability to recuperate quickly.

Hard hands

Hands that are hard as steel belong to dedicated workers, the sort who don't seem to lose a single day's work in their lives through physical ill-health. However, these emotionally unyielding types may be insensitive and are prone to the kinds of psychological disorders associated with repressing their feelings.

Very soft, doughy hands

This is the type of flabby hand that feels like a ball of uncooked pastry. It denotes an indolent, self-indulgent individual who generally has little physical energy or robustness. With illness, it is also associated with an imbalance of the thyroid gland.

Podgy hands

Obesity often appears in the hands in the form of very podgy basal phalanges to the fingers. This, too, indicates indolence and sensuality. A sensible general diet will also help to slim these fingers. More difficult to tackle are the little fatty deposits that are also found on the basal phalanges, but this time on the backs of the fingers. These show that the weight problem is a long-standing affair, which needs more rigorous treatment.

Podgy basal phalanges

Fatty deposits on back of basal phalanges

Supple hands

Flexible hands reflect a flexible, tolerant, laid-back nature. More able to adjust mentally, physically and emotionally to the demands of a situation, they can ride life's storms and are less vulnerable to serious diseases.

Stiff hands

Naturally stiff hands (not those stiffened by disease) suggest pent-up tension, or people who drive themselves too hard. These people may be prone to stress-related diseases such as hypertension (high blood pressure) and other cardiovascular conditions, for example.

Skin texture

When it comes to skin texture, the finer it appears and the more delicate the general feel of your hand, the weaker the emotional and physical constitution and immune system. The rougher and coarser your skin and hand, the more robust you are and the more resistant to disease. A very coarse hand can highlight a lack of sensitivity. Rough, dry hands can be one of the symptoms of an underactive thyroid, whereas shiny, smooth hands may indicate the opposite condition, hyperthyroidism, an overactive thyroid gland.

Colour and temperature

The colour of our hands, as well as any unnatural discoloration of the skin, can give vital clues about our health – and reveal some of our habits! Degrees of heat and cold, together with excessive moisture or dryness, are also tell-tale signs. In certain cases, hand temperature may give a good insight into the state of the endocrine (glandular) system. Although the normal temperature may vary from one individual to another, the ideal healthy hand should not be too hot nor too cold, not too dry nor too moist.

The language of gesture

As soon as you step into the consulting room, an astute doctor will immediately start to assess your psychological state by looking at your body language, including how you use your hands – whether you hold them limply or use animated gestures, hold them in a relaxed pose or make little nervous movements.

Psychologists confirm that our gestures are one of the first giveaway clues to our state of mind. What they have found is that, because most of our reactions are autonomic, we should trust our eyes in preference to our ears (that is, what you tell them is the matter with you)! From the health point of view, then, our gestures may reveal a good deal more about how we are feeling mentally than we might be able to describe in words.

Health notes

Nervousness or anxiety may be conveyed through urgent little hand movements such as hand-wringing, constantly playing with a strand of hair or incessant fiddling with a necklace or ring. These type of movements, however, are distinctly different from the involuntary tremors that are symptomatic of a variety of illnesses.

The four hand types

Just as, genetically, we might be classified as blond, brunette or redhead, which some would say reflects a great deal about our personalities, so, too, to the trained hand analyst, our hands can be classified into one of four types. Each type gives a good deal of information about what makes us tick. Once the general type has been established we then have a route into analysing the specific in terms of skin markings and line formation.

The Earth hand

Appearance
Squarish palm topped by short, blunt-tipped fingers. There are likely to be few lines in the palm – only three or four in many cases – but these will be strong, giving the hand an uncluttered look and a feeling of positive strength. Arched or looped fingerprints invariably go with this type.

Temperament and way of life
Traditional at heart: solid, stable and down-to-earth. Practical, hard-working and level-headed, these people like an orderly life. Outdoor rural types, fond of physical activity, they hate being inside for long and have a natural affinity for nature. Doggedly persistent, they have no time for fanciful schemes.

The Air hand

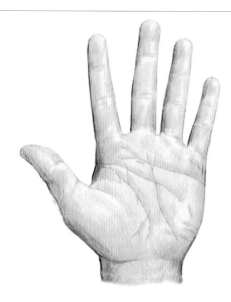

Appearance
A square palm and long fingers. The palm will contain several lines – at least a good few more than the bare essentials – and these will be clear and well-defined. Looped fingerprints are the predominant pattern. All in all, the Air hand has about it a certain 'wiry' look.

Temperament and way of life
Air-handed people have lively, inquisitive minds that make them eternal students, always eager to learn. Their mercurial mentality thrives on communication, variety and buzz. Chatty and friendly, their minds constantly tick over and, as quick learners, they have a short attention span and a low boredom threshold.

Elemental types

These four hand categories – named after the elements of Earth, Air, Fire and Water – are 'pure' types. Few hands will correspond to them exactly (after all, each hand is uniquely individual – not even our right hands match our left ones perfectly), but they should more or less conform to one type. If your hand falls between two categories, it simply means that you possess a combination of qualities. Read up on the descriptions of both types you think your hand combines, and then decide which set of characteristics suit your character and nature best.

The Fire hand

Appearance

Short fingers, but a longer palm than the Earth hand. A goodly amount of strong lines and whorled fingerprints.

Temperament and way of life

Physically super-dynamic, these people are always on the go, needing adventure and excitement and often channelling their energy into sports. The life and soul of the party, they are wonderful with people, spreading enthusiasm wherever they go. These high-profile types often become performers and entertainers. Happiest in the fast lane, they have a tendency to burn the candle at both ends and push themselves to their mental and physical limits.

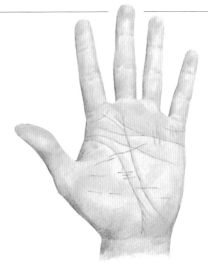

The Water hand

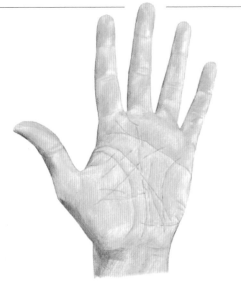

Appearance

Long, often lean and graceful, this hand characteristically has an oblong palm topped by long, tapering fingers. The palm is invariably covered by many fine lines. Loop fingerprint patterns are common.

Temperament and way of life

The most sensitive and gentle type. Poetic and romantic, they are artistic and musically gifted. Cultured and refined, they have good taste but tend to be unworldly, living with their heads in the clouds. This beautiful hand reflects an elegant body, so many are in the fashion, modelling and beauty industries, as well as the arts. Highly strung, these people are best in a peaceful, harmonious environment.

Fingers and thumbs

Human beings are the only creatures to possess such amazingly articulate fingers and highly developed thumbs. This unique combination enables us to make and create as we do, explaining our development and technological success. For hand analysts, the digits play an important role in assessing an individual's character and abilities.

Finger length

Fingers are classified as short or long, although this classification is always based on their length relative to the palm. To establish this correspondence, the middle finger is measured from its tip to the point where it meets the palm. The palm is in turn measured from this join to the top crease at the wrist and the two measurements are then compared. If the finger is at least three-quarters the length of the palm, the digits are considered 'long'. Shorter than this, they are classified as 'short'.

Long fingers are a sign of the painstaking worker, someone who pays attention to detail. These people tend to be slow and methodical, concentrating on doing one task at a time. In contrast, people with short fingers take in the whole at a glance. This makes them fast workers, good jugglers and excellent organizers, although they are prone to cut a few corners when it suits them.

The thumbs

Of all the digits, the thumbs are the most important indicators of psychological strengths and weaknesses. The thumb must balance the hand both in its shape and length. Too short on a long palm suggests lack of confidence and personal power. One that dominates the palm reveals someone who lacks subtlety and who may be overly aggressive. A thumb that looks 'comfortable' against the palm and fingers reveals vitality, staying power and common sense.

Thumb shape
A short and thick thumb indicates a lot of energy and determination, but not such good reasoning powers. You could be looking at a dominant, strong-willed personality. A person who has a ruthless streak, or who has a very nasty temper, often has a thick and bulbous thumb tip.

A short and narrow thumb reveals indecisiveness, a person who is easily swayed, possibly submissive – especially if the thumb also appears to look weaker than the rest of the hand.

If the second phalanx is narrow and hourglass-shaped, the individual is discreet and tactful. As thick as the top section, however, implies someone for whom 'a spade is a spade'.

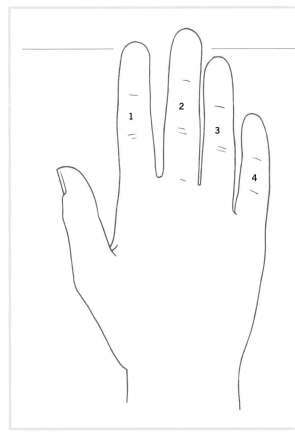

Individual fingers

1 The index finger symbolizes the self and reveals how an individual views themself. A confident person with plenty of self-esteem will possess a straight, up-standing index finger. If it's longer than the middle finger, that person has a domineering nature. If it's shorter, it suggests an inferiority complex.

2 The middle finger denotes our sense of responsibility. Ideally, this will be slightly longer than its neighbours either side, and held upright. As such, it reveals a person with a good sense of duty. Much longer, it suggests a morbid nature, and possible depression. Much shorter reveals unconventionality and irresponsibility.

3 The ring finger describes a person's creativity and personal satisfaction in life. If this finger towers over the middle finger, it's a sign of a dreamer and gambler. A very short finger suggests a philistine attitude with little cultural appreciation.

4 The little finger represents our abilities in business, science and communications. If this is noticeably longer than the rest, it reveals a witty, articulate nature. Very short suggests difficulties in expressing oneself both verbally and sexually.

Normal thumb proportion

Short, thick thumb

Short, narrow thumb

Narrow second phalanx

Nail form and shape

The nails also have a vivid health story to tell. Merely at a glance, badly chewed nails will suggest a nervous disposition, and brown-stained indices may give away a heavy smoker. Any hiccup, whether organic or nutritional, chronic or acute, will in some way register itself in the actual fabric of the nails, made sensitive by the rich blood supply beneath. Abnormal growth, furrowing, pitting, splitting or discoloration are some of the ways in which diseases, both of a temporary or long-term nature, will leave their marks.

Here may be found some pretty impressive clues concerning the cardiovascular system, glandular functioning and nutritional balance, as well as all manner of problems that might afflict us psychologically. Poor nutrition in particular affects nail development and so shows up very clearly in a range of abnormalities.

Nail shape

It has been recognized over the centuries that the shape of our nails reflects our temperament. And it is that temperament that describes our physical constitution, that colours our view of life, governs our interaction with others, affects how we deal with events and circumstances, and generally highlights our mental and emotional well-being.

Broadly speaking, shapes may be broken into three main categories:

- square (stable character type, with some notable exceptions)
- fan shape (sensitive and highly strung type)
- long (physically delicate and exhibits a lot of nervous energy)

However, each category may be subdivided still further. While the size of the nail must be viewed in relation to the size of the hand itself, as a general rule (when correlating nail shape to temperament) the smaller the nail, the more critical and narrow-minded the individual's outlook on life. People with small nails have a greater tendency towards cardiovascular problems, especially from middle age on. The larger the nail, the more even-tempered, placid and broad-minded the nature. Health problems with this type may tend towards nervous or psychological disorders. See Part Two, page 52, for more in-depth information.

Square

Fan shape

Long

Early warning signs

Here are some of the nail characteristics that may indicate health problems of various types. For in-depth analysis, turn to pages 53–4.

▲ Concave nail
Characterized by a pronounced dished or spooned appearance, commonly due to nutritional deficiencies.

▲ Convex nail
Characterized by a marked curvature of the nail whereby the tip of the nail wraps itself over and around the tip of the finger; can indicate respiratory disorders.

▲ Humped nail
A more serious condition than the curved nail because, whereas with the former it is only the tip that curves over, here the tissues of the nail bed become swollen so that the whole nail humps or rises upwards from the cuticle, giving the whole nail a rather bulbous look.

Pitting, thickening and brittle nails
Noticeable pitting can indicate auto-immune system problems; thick, tough nails, possibly yellow, show cardiovascular or lymphatic problems; and brittle nails may be a lack of calcium.

Moons
Like so many other features of the hand, the type, shape and colour of the moons may well be inherited and thus bring along with them any genetic predisposition to disease.

Colour of nail bed
Just as with skin pigmentation, the colour of the nail bed (the part that shows through the horny layer that constitutes the nail) reflects the state of the vascular system. Specks and spots can often indicate a mineral or vitamin deficiency.

▲ Horizontal ridging
Characterized by horizontal dents or grooves in the nails, sometimes occurring singly and sometimes forming a series of corrugations from cuticle to tip. Grabbing a sandwich as you rush off to those important meetings each afternoon, living off chips and processed food, experiencing a trauma, or deciding to go on a sudden crash diet, may all leave their imprint in the form of horizontal ridges.

▶ Vertical ridging
Characterized by ribs within the very fabric of the nail itself that feel bumpy when you run your thumbnail across them. These ridges are also caused by irregular production of the nail tissue. Vertical ridging can be hereditary, showing possible health problems, and distinct ridging on all the nails is linked to rheumatoid arthritis.

Nails and health

As long ago as the third century BCE, Hippocrates, Greek scholar and the father of medicine, recognized the value of the development and shape of the nails in reflecting disease. For Hippocrates, nail coloration in particular was a window to an individual's health. Too red suggested to him a dangerously choleric disposition; too white, a phlegmatic constitution. Modern scientific research has backed up many of his original theories, showing that the nail's delicate growth process is sensitive to the minutest physiological changes.

What nails are made of

Nails are made of a protein material called keratin, found throughout the animal kingdom as hair, claws, feathers, and even hooves and rhinos' horns. The function of the nail is primarily a protective one, guarding the nerve-rich, sensitive tip of the finger against injury.

The manufacture of the nail is an ongoing process, each nail taking roughly six months to grow from cuticle to quick – the end of the pink 'living' part of the nail. The free edge, or white tip, grows out from the 'matrix', or nail bed; because it is detached from the living cells, it may be cut or manicured as desired. In all assessments of the nails it is to the quick, and not the white tip, that the information applies. It is because the nails are continually being made that they respond so instantly to any hiccups in their growth process (interruptions to the blood supply, poor diet, a sudden shock that rocks the nervous system), registering the complaint either in the actual fabric of the nail or in the pigmentation of the bed beneath.

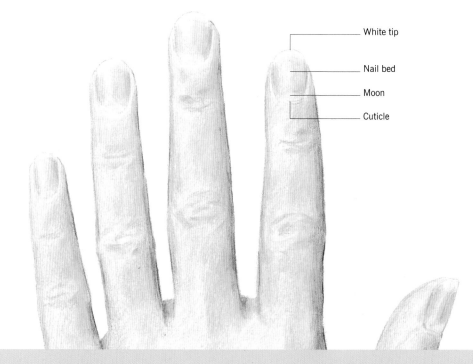

White tip

Nail bed

Moon

Cuticle

How nails are made

Production of the nail takes place below the surface of the finger, approximately 7–8 millimetres (¼ in) beyond the cuticle. Gently press the base of your thumbnail and you will notice a corresponding slight depression in the finger where the nail plate continues towards its root. This is where the nail begins to form, soft and gel-like at first, then hardening into compressed layers as it pushes its way out over the end of the digit.

Sensitive blood supply

As the nail grows out over the nail bed, the horny layers become transparent. The familiar pinkness of nails is actually due to blood-rich capillaries in the bed beneath, which nourishes the nail. It is essentially because of its sensitivity to the underlying blood supply that the nail's condition is such a good health register. If the blood supply is deficient in any way, it will instantly have a bearing on how the nail grows. Both injury and illness, then, may result in the abnormal development, deformities and obvious discoloration of our fingernails.

Cuticles and moons

Around its edge, each nail is protected by a flap of skin called the cuticle, which acts as an air-tight shield stopping dirt and infection from invading the delicate growth mechanism beneath. The milky white semi-circular moon, or lunule, at the nail's base is part of the dense growing root. Moons are more commonly seen on thumbs and less frequently on the little fingers. Their size and colour add to the nail's diagnostic properties.

Health notes

The rate of nail growth differs according to a range of factors. For a start, our toenails grow at a quarter the rate of our fingernails. When we are young our nails grow faster than when we are old. In the warmer weather of summertime they put on a greater spurt than they do in the winter. Right-handers amongst us will find that they have to file down the nails on their right hands more frequently than those on their left (and vice versa for left-handers). And even our middle and index fingernails seem to outpace those on our ring and little fingers, though it's our thumbnails that grow faster than all the rest.

◄ **Red fingernails**
Predisposition to poor circulation

Pale fingernails ▶
May indicate iron deficiency

Fingerprints

The distinctive skin patterns known as 'papillary ridges' form part of the top layer of skin that covers the palms of our hands and the soles of our feet. In scientific circles, this system of ridges is called dermatoglyphics – *derma*, meaning 'skin', and *glyph*, 'a carving'. Looked at close-up, the ridging resemblzes sheets of corrugated iron with lines and furrows running parallel to one another. However, here and there the corrugations swirl themselves into complex patterns of loops, whorls and arches. These are most commonly recognized on the fingertips, as our fingerprints (see opposite). A classification system has evolved from these patterns, and measurements are taken between these ridges (see below).

The condition, formation and location of these patterns can provide much invaluable information about well-being and state of health. As with the nails, information gleaned from skin ridges should never be used on its own as a means of diagnosis but should be used as a tool in conjunction with other clinical data to confirm a medical condition that is already suspected.

Medical evidence

Medical research has turned its attention on skin ridges and fingerprints in an attempt to match particular patterns to specific disorders. All dermal patterns are genetically inherited and already formed by the fourth month of foetal development. Any inherited abnormality or hiccup in the developmental process imprints itself as abnormal papillary ridging. For example, babies whose mothers contract rubella (German measles) during the first month or so of gestation run over a fifty per cent risk of being born with major defects, and the skin markings in their hands will reflect those abnormalities. Scientific findings confirm a link between ridge patterns and chromosomal abnormalities – the best-documented correlation so far being between abnormal patterns and Down's syndrome.

Measuring ridges

Both for forensic and medical purposes it is necessary to measure the size and quantity of ridges that constitute a fingerprint. Such measurements are achieved by drawing a line from the apex of the 'triradius' (a triangular formation created when three sets of ridges meet) to the central core of the skin pattern, and counting the ridges in between (see right). This is known as the 'ridge count', used in forensic analysis to make an absolute match between prints collected at scenes of crime and the suspected criminal's fingerprints. In medical research, the ridge count is a critical factor when comparisons are made between normal and abnormal hands.

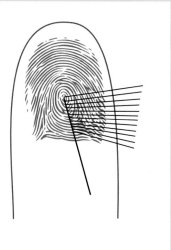

Fingerprint patterns

Loops, whorls and arches are the three main categories of fingerprint patterns, although two further types derived from these – the tented arch and the composite – bring the total classification to five. Years of matching patterns to their owners have brought to light distinctive personality characteristics associated with each category. And these character traits will have a direct bearing on the mental and physical state of the individual's health.

The whorl
Intense individualists

The arch
Hard-working, practical and reserved

The loop
Versatile, flexible and adaptable

◀ **Composite**
Just as with the tented arch, it is rare to find a complete set of composite patterns. When this fingerprint is present, it will more usually be found on the thumbs and indices. Composite patterns suggest a mentality that needs to see all sides of the picture.

Tented arch ▶
It is rare to find a whole set of tented arches. In general, these tend to occur only on the index or middle fingers. When present, they denote enthusiasm and sensitivity.

Other skin markings

Apart from fingerprint patterns, there are other lines that may be found on the fingers. These markings have various health implications that can be further defined according to the finger on which they appear.

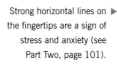

Strong horizontal lines on ▶ the fingertips are a sign of stress and anxiety (see Part Two, page 101).

◀ Strong vertical lines on the fingertips are a sign of imbalance in the glands (see Part Two, page 102).

Strong vertical lines on the ▶ two bottom phalanges of the fingers are a warning of possible exhaustion (see Part Two, page 103).

Features of the Palms

The mounts

The padding on your hand is distributed in the form of little 'cushions' called mounts. Because mounts are believed to represent storehouses of vitality, their condition highlights your salient personality and state of health. The mounts are named after the planets, and those who know anything about classical mythology will recognize the meanings behind the names.

Under- and over-development

Apart from the Venus mount, usually the most pronounced, and the Saturn mount, normally the least developed, an ideally well-balanced person has fairly equally padded mounts. However, most hands possess unequal mounts. Dominant ones signal your salient characteristics, but any that are unusually large or small suggest an over-abundance or notable lack of the qualities represented by that area. If there are two apparently dominant mounts, the qualities of each are prominently combined. In totally flat hands, it will be factors such as fingerprints or lines in the palm that will hold the health clues.

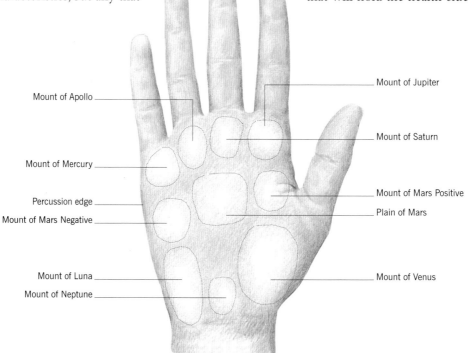

Mount of Apollo

Mount of Mercury

Percussion edge

Mount of Mars Negative

Mount of Luna

Mount of Neptune

Mount of Jupiter

Mount of Saturn

Mount of Mars Positive

Plain of Mars

Mount of Venus

The principal mounts

Top of palm

Mount of Jupiter
Located just beneath your index (or Jupiter) finger.

Mount of Saturn
Located just beneath your middle (or Saturn) finger.

Mount of Apollo
Located just beneath your ring (or Apollo) finger. This mount may be skewed slightly towards the little finger and merged with the Mercury mount. If these two mounts appear dominant, their qualities will be jointly manifested.

Mount of Mercury
Located directly beneath your little (or Mercury) finger, at the percussion edge of the hand. This area is often merged into the mount of Apollo, and so represents both sets of qualities.

Middle/base of palm

Mount of Mars Positive
Located above the Venus mount, tucked under the wing of the thumb. When your thumb is pressed into the side of the palm, this mount forms a neat little hump. Where it is large and hard, and causes the Life line (see page 68) to sweep out wide, the mount is deemed over-developed. Where there is little development, so there is either a dip or the skin forms empty wrinkles when the thumb is pressed into the edge of the palm, the mount is then judged to be deficient.

Mount of Mars Negative
Located on the percussion edge. Because it is continuous with the Luna mount, the two are often indistinguishable from one another. If the mount is well-developed, it might push out the side of the palm to form a curved percussion edge.

Plain of Mars
The central expanse of palm that lies between the mounts of Mars Positive and Mars Negative.

Mount of Venus
Also known as the thenar eminence, it is located directly below your thumb, forming the 'ball' of the thumb. It is bounded by the semi-circular Life line. When the mount is large, the Life line may sweep out towards the centre of the palm. When meagre, the line may hug the root of the thumb closely. In most hands this is the biggest mount and should not as a rule be interpreted as dominant, unless it towers above the rest or covers a huge expanse of palm.

Mount of Luna
Also called the hypothenar eminence, it is located low on the percussion edge of the hand, just above the wrist. It may be developed outwards, pushing out the side of the palm, or low down, forming a knob just above the wrist. When it is as large or larger than a normally developed Venus mount, it is considered over-developed. When it is lean, it is deemed under-developed.

Mount of Neptune
Not found on all hands, it lies at the palm base, between Venus and Luna. When developed, it appears as a high padded point joining the two mounts; more often, it resembles a valley between them.

Skin-ridge patterns

A free-flowing arrangement of skin ridges is commonly found on the mounts of Venus and Luna, although loops, whorls and arches also occur on these areas and also on the palm just below the base of the digits (see illustration on page 61 for more detail). Of particular health interest are the Luna patterns. Research shows that an increased incidence of complex patterns here may occur in those with psychological problems.

The major lines

The general appearance of the lines in our palms, their condition, construction and composition, give invaluable clues about our mental and physical well-being.

The major lines are known as the Life, Heart, Head and Fate lines. Studies show that the first three develop in that order, around the fourth month of foetal development – roughly at the same time as the skin-ridge patterns. It is believed that any chromosomal abnormalities that mark the ridge patterns may also affect the construction of the main lines at this stage of development. So, like fingerprints, the major lines will also be influenced by the DNA package that we inherit from our parents. The Fate line may develop later on, and many babies are born without it, but develop it some years after birth. However, there are just as many babies who are born with a complete set of major – and minor – lines.

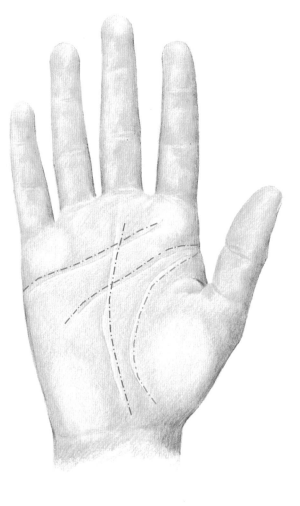

| — · — · — · — | Heart | — · — · — · — | Fate |
| — · — · — · — | Head | — · — · — · — | Life |

Energy channels

Think of the lines in your hands as channels conducting energy – rather like electric wiring in your house. If this wiring system breaks down, your appliances will fail when you need them. In fact, you may blow a fuse when you overload the system or, worse still, the wiring may spark a fire and burn the house down. And so lines that are thin, frayed or broken can be a sign of danger and need to be dealt with as soon as possible.

The practised palmist can spot signs of neglect long before problems develop, even well in advance of a stethoscope or blood test picking up trouble. Like wiring, the body takes time to fail. And, because lines change, taking preventive action as soon as we detect signs may make all the difference. Good diet, adequate exercise, plenty of rest and a positive attitude will help to keep those channels in good working order.

Comparing lines

Comparing the strength of the major lines is always a revealing exercise. In some people, the main lines are equally balanced, but in others one line may stand out from the rest, whether because it is stronger, deeper or wider, or perhaps of a slightly different colour. A strong Life line shows physical stamina – expected in the hand of an athlete, for example. A strong Head line, however, suggests that mental energies are the driving force. These people must not let their busy minds push their bodies too far. Where the Heart line is emphasized, its owner tends to let their heart rule their head. Here, impulsiveness may lead not only to mental and physical exhaustion, but also to accidents and injuries.

Health notes

Though formed so early on, our lines do change throughout the course of our lives. According to the way we live our lives, to our environmental conditioning, to the decisions we take, and to our states of health, our lines can grow, increase in number, change colour, strengthen, weaken, diminish and (in some cases) even disappear altogether. Some changes may take years to come about, while others – such as stress lines across the fingertips – can appear and disappear again within a matter of days.

Markings on the lines

The major – and minor – lines often have markings on them that add to their significance.

Breaks in the line: change and transition

Crossbar: normally represents obstructions of some kind

Star (made from a starburst-shaped cluster of tiny crossbars): a shock to the system

Island: a lowering of energy levels

Chain (a series of islands): denotes low vitality levels

Square (made from four lines): has various meanings
(see Part Two, pages 74–5)

Fraying/tasselling: seen towards the end of a line; can denote a scattering of energies

Spots/dots/indentations: suggest tension or stress

Life, Head and Heart lines

The Life line

Contrary to old wives' tales, the Life line does not indicate longevity. This line denotes the quality of our lives. It records our genetic inheritance and our awareness of our physical strength and general health.

Anything that is likely to sap our strength, or affect us physically or psychologically in such a way that our health comes under attack, is registered throughout this line by specific negative markings such as chains and crossbars. A strong, healthy line represents the essential springboard from which all other activity in life can take place.

The Head line

The belief that our thoughts generate tremendous power is succinctly put in the phrase 'mind over matter'. And when it comes to health we all know how easy it is to talk ourselves into feeling a good deal better or worse. Our experiences of fear, anxiety, stress or pain can all be modified by our expectations of a situation. This is shown in the Head line.

The Heart line

This represents our emotions – how we feel about ourselves and other people. On the psychological side, it reflects how we relate to others; physiologically, it reveals specific information about the circulatory and cardiovascular system, and about the body's biochemistry. As with all the lines, the direction and the formation of the line are as important as each other in building up a health profile.

———— Life	———— Head	———— Heart

Locating the Life line

The Life line is the semi-circular line that sweeps around the thumb. In some hands it hugs tightly around the base of the thumb, while in others it makes a broad arc out towards the centre of the palm. It begins on the edge of the palm somewhere between the thumb and index finger and proceeds down the hand and around to end at the base of the palm near the wrist.

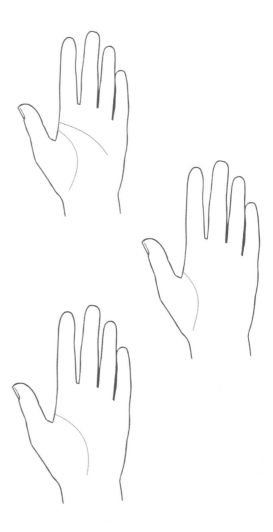

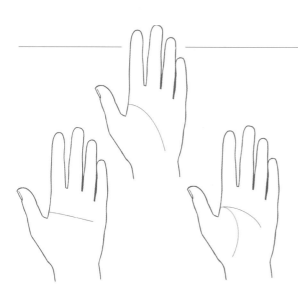

Locating the Head line

Working down from the fingers, the Head line is the second horizontal crease that cuts across the centre of the palm. In some hands it takes a straight course; in others, it forms a gentle curve. The Head line may also slope downwards sharply, to end almost touching the wrist at the opposite edge of the palm. Sometimes the line may begin attached to the Life line, or perhaps start from the mount of Mars, inside the Life line. Or it may take its root higher up in the palm, completely detached from the Life line and forming a wide gap between the two.

Locating the Heart line

The Heart line lies horizontally across the top of the palm and is the first line one encounters when working down from the fingers. Some Heart lines are lower down than others, some are curved, whilst others are straight. These differences distinguish the different ways in which people relate to others.

Start and finish
The Heart line begins at the percussion edge, sweeps out towards the thumb and terminates in a variety of ending points. (There is controversy over this. More traditional hand analysts believe that the Heart line begins beneath the index finger and swings out in the direction of the percussion edge. Others, including myself, think the opposite.) Wherever it ends, whether beneath the middle finger or the index, whether it travels straight across or up to touch the base of the digits, gives important insights. However, it is the construction and composition of this line, together with any markings found upon it,

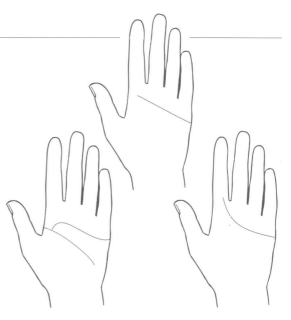

that registers the functioning of the heart and blood vessels. And this information is mainly contained within the first four centimetres (one-and-a-half inches) or so of the line where it passes beneath the little and ring fingers, because this is the area that governs the heart and lungs.

The Fate line

As mentioned earlier, the Fate line may not develop until sometime after birth. There are even people who never develop a Fate line at all, though it should be stressed that this is nothing to worry about!

No matter when it appears, its presence denotes the beginnings of a sense of stability, responsibility and putting down roots, whether physically or metaphorically. Running up the middle of the palm as it does, it might be looked upon as a central ridge pole, so that its strength or weakness, its solidity or fragmentation, its degree of straightness or crookedness, corresponds to the amount of stability, security and good sense that we feel we possess in our lives.

Locating the Fate line

Of all the lines, the Fate is somewhat of a maverick. It is read from the wrist up towards the fingers but can have a variety of starting points in the palm and an equal variety of endings. Sometimes it spans the whole length of the palm, maybe appearing only for a short while and then disappearing again altogether.

Root of the matter

The line may take root from the centre of the palm at the wrist, may begin attached to the Life line, originate from the mount of Luna or

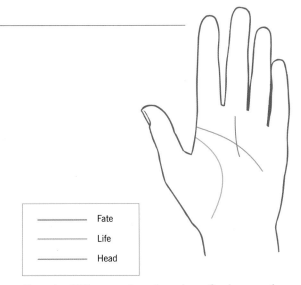

————	Fate
————	Life
————	Head

form itself from various locations further up the palm. Its designated ending is on the mount of Saturn, beneath the middle finger, although it may swing over to the Jupiter mount, beneath the index, or the other way to end on the Apollo mount, beneath the ring finger. It may also peter out well before reaching the top of the palm or else come to rest at the Head or Heart lines.

Fortunately, the Fate line can be timed (see page 89) fairly accurately, so starting and ending points, as well as onset and duration of markings, can be assessed with confidence.

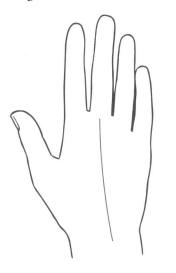

Supporting role

The notion of the Fate line as a ridge pole also helps to explain its other function, which is so important from the medical viewpoint. This is its role as a support, principally to the Life line, but also to the lines of Head and Heart.

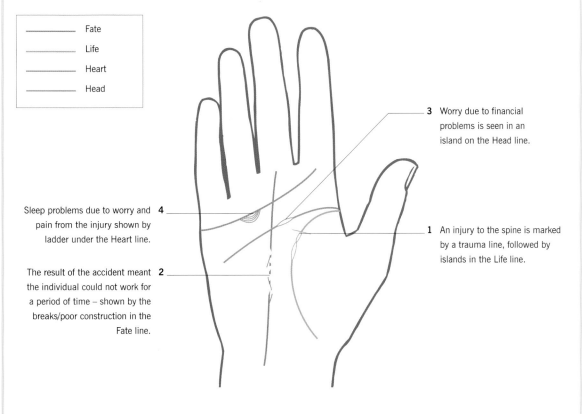

——— Fate
——— Life
——— Heart
——— Head

3 Worry due to financial problems is seen in an island on the Head line.

Sleep problems due to worry and pain from the injury shown by ladder under the Heart line. **4**

1 An injury to the spine is marked by a trauma line, followed by islands in the Life line.

The result of the accident meant the individual could not work for a period of time – shown by the breaks/poor construction in the Fate line. **2**

Helpful correspondences
If, for instance, the Life line is patchy, thin or adversely marked at any point, a strong Fate line at the corresponding time can bolster up any weaknesses implied, shoring up the breach in our physical defences. Such a reciprocal relationship also exists between the Head and Fate lines. A patch of multiple Fate lines, for example, representing a frenetic burst of activity, might find its correspondence in a fluffy stretch of Head line, denoting stress from over-work. Alternatively, a depression mark in the latter might highlight the results of an island in the former, suggesting, say, that its owner's dissatisfaction with work at that time is a serious problem.

Cross-referencing
This is why it is essential that the lines are constantly cross-referenced, balanced against each other, compared and contrasted at every stage of analysis. And with none more so than the Fate line, with its central, supporting role – this reflector and enlightener of events, register of mental, physical and emotional detail, supporter and sustainer, this central ridge pole upon which hangs a representation of our aspirations and driving force, our ability to take charge of our lives and destinies.

The minor lines

There are all kinds of minor lines on the hand that also speak volumes about our psychological and physical well-being. The one that is especially helpful where our health is concerned has to be the Hepatica or Liver line, best known as the Health line. However, it cannot be stressed enough that all lines are important and have a role to play, no matter how big or how small, to the whole pattern of our health. So ancillary lines like the Girdle of Venus or the Via Lascivia act as individual pieces of the jigsaw that must be interpreted in order to see a clearer picture of the whole.

The Health line

There is a good deal of confusion surrounding this line, not least because historically it has been known by a variety of different names. The Liver line, the Via Hepatica, the Mercury line are just a few of its alternative titles, depending very much on which book on the subject you are likely to pick up. Additionally, it may also be referred to as the Stomach or Spleen line and herein lies a clue as to its significance, because one of its major roles is to reflect the body's digestive functioning and eliminative

—·—·—·— Health	—·—·—·— Apollo	
—·—·—·— Allergy	—·—·—·— Girdle of Venus	

processes. When these two functions are operating efficiently, the body is in a healthy state of being. But, when digestion is sluggish, the whole system feels decidedly off.

Although the Health line is not always present in a hand, if you happen to possess one, it tells that you have a heightened awareness of your body mechanics. It shows that you are the sort of person who is conscious of every twinge, every ache, every heartbeat, every slight change in temperature.

The Girdle of Venus

The presence in a hand of the Girdle of Venus tells of heightened sensitivity. It is perhaps more favourable when the marking is found in fragments, because a complete semi-circle denotes an individual who is especially nervous and, in extreme cases, susceptible to neurosis.

The Allergy line

The Via Lascivia, otherwise known as the poison line, is now called the Allergy line, and – as the name implies – indicates a sensitivity to allergens. Those who possess this line may experience adverse reactions to certain foodstuffs, chemicals or alcohol.

The Apollo line

A well-marked Apollo line is a sign of personal contentment and satisfaction. It also reveals a sunny outlook and happy disposition and, since attitude plays a vital role in health, possessing this line is a plus factor for its owner's well-being.

Flaring

This is the term for fine, oblique lines that arise in the centre of the hand. They point in the direction of the ring and little fingers and suggest digestive disorders.

Health notes

A formation of lines known as the Medical Stigmata is made up of three oblique lines with (sometimes) one crossing line, and is located high on the palm directly beneath the ring and little fingers. When present, the marking reflects a natural, inherent gift for healing (see Part Two, page 100).

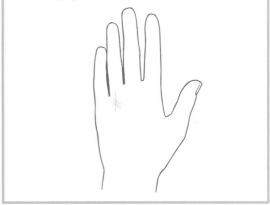

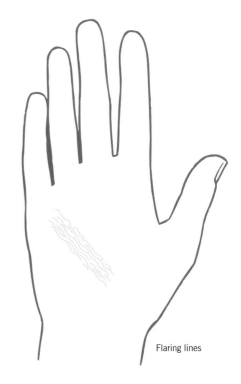

Flaring lines

Locating the Health line

The Health line, if it occurs at all in the hand, is normally found on the ulna side of the palm – that is, towards the percussion edge. It may take its root from several places but it normally runs diagonally from the base of the palm towards the little finger. In some hands it may strike the Life line; in others it cuts through it and runs into the mount of Venus. It may also shoot up from the mount of Luna, and can sometimes stretch from the base of the palm to the fingers.

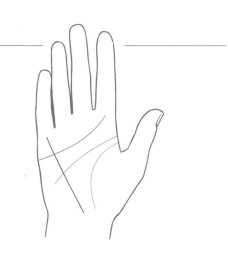

Locating the Girdle of Venus

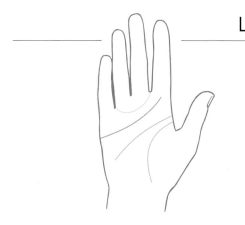

In its most prominent form, the Girdle of Venus is a semi-circular line found at the top of the hand between the Heart line and the base of the fingers. It enters the palm from the webbing between the first two fingers and sweeps its way across and up, to end on the web between the ring and little fingers.

Locating the Allergy line

The line, when present, is found lying in a horizontal position fairly low down on the palm. It enters the hand from the percussion edge and proceeds across the mount of Luna towards the Life line.

	Life		Heart		Girdle of Venus
	Head		Health		Allergy

Other considerations

Matching lines to hand types

Just as a pair of shoes must suit and, more importantly, fit you well, so lines in the palm must both suit and fit the type of hand in which they occur. The four different categories of hands – Earth, Air, Fire and Water (see pages 16–17) – are each associated with particular types, qualities and formations of lines.

Where the lines suit the hand type, an easy relationship will exist between mind, body and spirit. But, like an ill-fitting pair of shoes that pinch and chafe, where the lines mismatch, that relationship may not be quite so comfortable. For example, too many fine and wispy lines in an Earth hand would be as ill-matched as too few very strong lines in a Water hand. Both would present a complex situation where the wiring and energy demands would be at variance with the needs of their owners.

Well-matched: strong lines in Earth hand

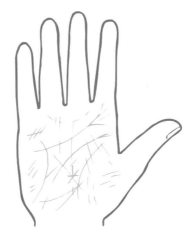

Ill-matched: fine wispy lines in Earth hand

Colour of lines

The colour of your lines should be slightly darker than your skin but should generally match in tone. European hands ideally contain dark-pink lines, black and Asian hands are graced with browny-beige lines set in pinkish-beige palms. However, care must be taken when making judgements about the colour of lines, for not only should the race of the owner be taken into account, but also the ambient temperature and, just as importantly, whatever activity has preceded the analysis. If you've been energetically working out in the gym, for example, you might expect that your lines, and the colour of your whole hand, will be a good deal pinker than if you've been defrosting your freezer for the past couple of hours. So please do use your common sense when you're making this assessment. For more detail, see page 94.

Full or empty?

Analysts also have to take into account whether a hand is 'empty' or 'full'. This refers to whether the hand is a veritable cobweb or just possesses a few clear lines. Put simplistically, the more lines a hand shows, the more sensitive and highly strung an individual is. The fewer the lines, the more robust the nervous system and, consequently, the less sensitive the disposition. Turn to page 103, for a detailed feature on the subject.

Reading the Hands

Getting down to business

This section discusses useful background information designed to help analysts find a helpful approach to hand-reading. Certain principles are suggested to make effective analysis easier and clearer.

Some historical background …

No one knows precisely when, or how, people began to read hands but one of the earliest documented references is found in sacred Indian texts from around the second millennium BCE. The emperors of Ancient China were using thumbprints as personal signatures on state documents as far back as 3000 BCE – five thousand years before English police 'discovered' the fingerprinting identification system, around 1900.

Dissatisfaction at work, as shown by islands in the Fate line, is compensated by a strong Apollo line, showing a rich and fulfilling creative life.

Over the intervening millennia, the art of hand-reading spread from the Far East through Ancient Greece and into Western Europe. The learned physicians Hippocrates and Galen made diagnostic findings about hand-markings that are still valid today. Plato, Homer and Aristotle, too, were versed in palmistry as a means of assessing character, as evidenced in Aristotle's *Chiromantia*.

Since then, hand-reading has had a chequered career, taught as a university subject in some countries and falling foul of Church and State in others. In northern Europe, Britain in particular, palmistry enjoyed a resurgence in the later 1800s, although the Victorians' taste for the macabre meant that they dwelt on the darker aspects – warnings of death and mayhem and gory features such as 'murderer's thumb'!

Health notes

Hand analysts today should be prepared to see very different signs in the hands from those of a few decades ago. For example, where many people once had 'jobs for life' and kept to much the same kind of predictable lifestyle throughout their days, life patterns have changed dramatically and are now much more fluid and shifting, involving a lot of change. This means that when analysts look at hands they now see a great many more broken Fate lines (the Fate line denotes change), whereas in the past they would have commonly only seen long, unbroken ones.

Modern methods

But it was the birth of psychoanalysis in the early twentieth century that helped produce a whole new way of interpreting the hand, based more on a psychological, individual character-based perspective. We also now acknowledge the roles of free will and change more readily (in our lives and in our hand-markings), believing that we can intervene to improve our situation – the markings are not irrevocable. In recent times, too, medical research has shown some strong correlations between health and hand-patterns, at last validating scientifically what was believed all those centuries ago.

A world of possibility

In hand analysis, as in life, there are few absolutes and it is essential to remember that any hand-markings simply denote potential, predisposition, possibility. Their mere presence does not imply that a certain event is bound to happen. Just as a doctor might advise a patient to head off a health problem by changing their diet, for example, the hand analyst can tell clients that, with a change of behaviour, attitude or lifestyle, there's a good chance that negative markings can disappear and lines repair themselves as the body's healing process takes place.

Making diagnoses

It must be emphasized at this point, in bold letters, that any negative signs in a major indicator such as the Heart line **must be backed up by other markings** in the major lines or by other recognized features in the hand and fingers before drawing any conclusions about the owner's health. And, if you are truly concerned, advise the person to consult a doctor.

Always remember that:
a) you might be quite wrong
b) the marking may be alluding to some psychological upset rather than to a clinical problem
c) it may simply be denoting a predisposition to an illness – rather than indicating a fully fledged clinical disease.

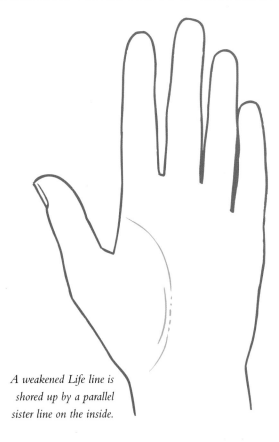

A weakened Life line is shored up by a parallel sister line on the inside.

Left or right?

One of the major issues you will have to deal with when reading hands is that of which hand is 'dominant'. Many people are confused about right- and left-handedness – no wonder when silly old wives' tales such as 'The left is what you're born with and the right is what you make of yourself' abound. And the fact that the word 'left' in Latin (*sinister/sinistra*) implies sinister malevolence has meant that for centuries left-handers have been blighted as untrustworthy, possibly villainous.

Redressing the balance

Fortunately, psychologists have done a sterling job in clearing up the whole issue of right- and left-handedness and, in the process, have completely vindicated the long-suffering left-hander. Research has found that roughly twelve to thirteen per cent of people in the Western world are left-handed, and of those slightly more tend to be male. More importantly, tests have shown that the two hemispheres of our brain control very different functions. The left side deals with what might be termed 'hard-core' subjects,

Public and private selves

The scientific findings with regard to left- and right-handedness also help to clarify the picture for hand analysts and confirm what we have known all along about the differences between the two hands. Each hand contains specific information – the passive hand (controlled by the 'intuitive', 'emotional' hemisphere) reveals our instinctive reactions, our potential, our private selves. The dominant hand (controlled by the 'logical', 'rational' hemisphere) tells us about our public selves, our persona, whether we have developed our full potential. We recognize that information may differ between the hands, and may even show some conflict.

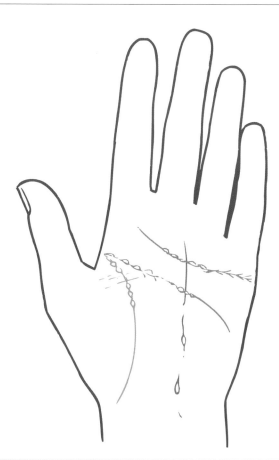

Broken and poorly formed lines in this left hand, and at the beginning of the main lines in this right hand, suggest a weakened constitution when young. Better health, and consequently stronger line development, occurred when the subject moved to a warmer country and better lifestyle in her early twenties.

such as the logical processes required to read, write and calculate. The right hemisphere, meanwhile, deals with the 'softer' processes – with our intuitive and emotional responses to different things, our ability to appreciate art, music and suchlike.

Crossing over

What is fascinating is that commands from these two sides of our brain cross over and control the opposite side of our bodies, so that our left hemisphere controls our right eye, ear, arm, hand, leg, foot and so on, while the right brain hemisphere controls our left side. And this is why the majority of us write with our right hands, kick a football with our right foot, and so on. Our right hand, then, becomes known as our dominant or active hand, whereas the left is our passive hand.

With left-handers, the only difference is that the roles of their two hemispheres are reversed. Instead, it is their right hemisphere that deals with the 'hard-core' subjects and controls their left sides – so their left hands become dominant. Simple as that, nothing more sinister.

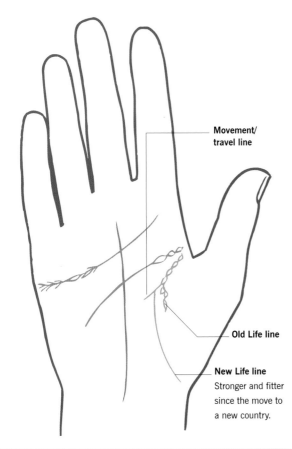

Movement/
travel line

Old Life line

New Life line
Stronger and fitter
since the move to
a new country.

Understanding the differences

Why it is so important to understand the differences between our two hands is that, when it comes to analysing the markings that specifically concern health matters, we must clearly differentiate between the two findings. Markings in our passive hands will tell us about our inherited predispositions to disease, what could happen if we were to abuse our systems. The markings in our active or dominant hands show the sort of illnesses that are more likely to develop.

Seeing the whole picture

However, the two hands must be taken together because there could just as well be positive markings in the passive hand that could offset any negative information found in the active one. When both hands show the same adverse marking, that is when the odds would seem stacked in favour of that particular illness taking place. But, even then, we cannot be sure because lines do change – in both hands.

Step-by-step guide

Here are some important principles designed to help you – both analyst and the person being analysed – get the most out of hand-reading.

Be a detective
Look upon hand analysis as similar to a police investigator putting together an Identikit of an individual. In general, features tend to blend with each other; it is those exceptional markings that you are seeking and that may need further careful study.

Spot early signs
Intervention is much more likely to be successful if you spot the signs in the hands early enough and keep monitoring them to keep pace with any changes.

Exercising your free will

One of the cardinal rules of hand analysis is that lines can and do change and that we all have free will that we can use to a greater or lesser extent in our lives.

If, by examining our hands, we discover that we have a tendency towards respiratory problems, say, then we may have the power to do something about it if we so wish. By keeping warm, perhaps, by avoiding chills, by not smoking or by seeking prompt medical attention the minute we feel a cold has gone to our chests, we can prevent any bronchial trouble from developing. But if we know we are predisposed to bronchitis and choose to live in a freezing, damp garret, chain-smoke and ignore any chest pains that occur, then the weakest link – here, the respiratory system – will pay the price.

Power in our hands
By studying our hands, and by measuring and timing the lines, we take control of our own fate, our own destiny, our own lives and our own health. It is by understanding the markings in our hands, and how these relate to the system as a whole, and by using our free will, that we are able to take that control.

Keep everything in proportion
In a car engine, all the components must be synchronized and function in harmony, otherwise the timing will be thrown out or one component will wear more rapidly than another, producing a domino effect as each part places undue stress on every other in turn.

And this idea holds true for palmistry because one of its most important underlying principles is that every aspect of a hand must be in good proportion to the others. A mount that is disproportionately large, a finger that is exceptionally short in comparison to the rest, a nail that stands out because it is a different shape, will emphasize the particular characteristic about you that is represented by that feature. An aspect that is discordant will, in a sense, throw the whole system out of balance. This also applies to your lines.

Do the lines match the hand type?
If yours do, you will be said to be well-balanced. If they don't, you may experience all sorts of tensions and conflicting emotions. You might find it difficult to take things in your stride, react inappropriately to certain situations or give out the wrong signals to other people. In extreme cases there may be what psychologists term 'behavioural problems', with all the aggression and sudden mood swings that go with a build-up of emotional frustration. Altogether, it is this very mismatching of the elements in the hand that reflects the internal friction that can undermine your mental and physical health if the tensions go unchecked.

Look at all the signs together
To summarize what we've said before, don't look at just one line, or one mount, and start drawing conclusions. All the features of both hands must be considered together to provide a well-balanced picture.

Check colour and construction
Another important factor in detecting any imbalance in your system is the actual colour of your lines. Too pale or too dark in comparison to the skin of your

palm would be symptomatic that all is not well. Also consider whether lines are thick or thin, very fine or deeply etched. Look at any faults or unexpected markings on them – whether they are frayed, broken, crossed, islanded, chained or damaged in any way – to home in on potential danger spots and raise the alarm.

Is the timing right?

Though not absolutely accurate to the minute, one of the great advantages of hand analysis is that these markings in your lines can be timed by measuring your palm and applying a timing gauge to it (this is explained in Part Two, see pages 88–89). So some forecasting can be made in the same way as a doctor predicts the possible onset of disease by noting specific early-warning symptoms. A close examination of markings in your lines will lead a hand analyst to conclude certain outcomes according to your current behaviour, habits and lifestyle. And by using the timing gauges, a pretty fair judgement can be made of when your system is likely to come under attack.

Work in good light

When making observations or taking measurements of skin patterns and fingerprints, always work in good light and try to view the hand under a magnifying glass. Except for just a cursory glance, it is easier to work from a print.

The power of touch

Don't be afraid to palpate the hand. Hold it, stroke it, massage it, if you feel it necessary to do so. What you need to ascertain is the hand's consistency, but remember, too, in the meantime that touch is a most powerful and therapeutic medium. Holding an individual's hand will tell you a lot about that person, and will also enable you to give a whole lot more to them. Because, whether you believe it or not, by holding that person's hand you will be exchanging energies and transmitting to your client precisely what they have come to you for – your healing powers.

1–2–3 of hand-health

Here's a quick three-step guide to analysing your hands, plus a reminder of the things you should be looking out for.

1 Check first that all features are in harmony. What category of hand is it and do the fingers suit the palm? Does the thumb balance the hand, or does it appear odd in comparison? Also ask if the finger and palmar patterns are normal, and whether the palm's lines suit the hand, depending on whether they are Earth, Air, Fire or Water types.

2 Take careful note of the course and direction of the lines, of their quality and construction. Check for details such as islands, breaks and branches. These will all need to be accurately timed, since they will give data on events, situations and circumstances in the past, present and possibly the future.

3 Next, compare one hand with the other. Use drawings to map the dominant and passive hands on top of each other, to take account of any discrepancies between them that would highlight a mismatch between that individual's private and public sides, and also between the 'actual' and 'potential' aspects of their lives.

SUMMARY OF WHAT TO LOOK FOR:

- Full/empty hand *(see page 103)*
- Matching lines to hand type *(see page 37)*
- Colour *(see page 50)*
- Construction of the lines *(see page 102)*
- Specific markings on the lines *(see page 74)*
- Timing *(see page 88)*

Part Two

Health Pointers

Specific Health Indicators

Now that you are familiar with the basics of palmistry, you can
begin to make a more detailed analysis of the health indicators that
can be identified in the hands. Building on what you have learned
in Part One, this section leads you on a point-by-point journey
through the undulating landscape and pathways of the palm. Here,
you will discover the specific physical and psychological health
markers represented by each area of the hand and learn about
their present effects – and their implications for the future. What
conditions are you particularly susceptible to? Are you suffering
from stress? Do you have a predisposition to migraine, back
problems or hypertension? Whether the indications reveal allergies
or digestive problems, nervous disorders or perhaps more serious
conditions such as heart problems, for example, your hands have
a great deal to tell you about your state of health.

Indications in the Hands

The hands' appearance

As outlined in Part One, gesture, hand–movement, temperature, colour and hand-type are all useful health indicators.

Gesture

- *Limply held* hands convey dejection and negativity, often seen in those who feel they lack control over their lives. Of course, physiologically, those who are seriously ill might also let their hands and arms fall limply because they simply lack physical strength.
- *The way the thumb is generally held* is very revealing. One that is held rigidly close to the palm, so as to form an acute angle, betrays someone who is over-controlled. Those who are inhibited or who suffer from inner conflicts or tensions may display this sort of rigidity. A more flexible thumb, one that forms a wider angle to the rest of the hand, or whose tip has a supple bend, reveals a much more open, easy-going disposition.
- *Perspiring* is one of the body's autonomic responses to fear. Because a vast number of sweat glands are concentrated in the palm, we have all experienced uncomfortably sweaty hands when we've been apprehensive. The most characteristic accompanying gesture is to wipe our hands – down the sides of our thighs, or perhaps with a tissue.
- *Jerky or rigid hand or arm movements* are invariably a sign of tension. So is fiddling. Drumming a tattoo on the table top, fingers fussing over the beads of a necklace, or twisting a strand of hair round and round an index finger – all of these are instantly recognizable signs of nervousness, lack of self-confidence or impatience. Another obvious sign of anxiety is hand-wringing.
- *Nail-biting* is associated with a sense of insecurity. In adults, badly bitten nails are a classic symptom of an anxious disposition.
- *Easily flowing, controlled movements,* with hands held calmly in a relaxed pose, convey confidence and self-assurance.

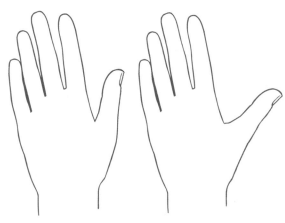

Thumb held close: signals inhibition or inner conflict

Thumb at wider angle: indicates open, easy-going disposition

- *Arms and hands that are held close to the body,* tucked into pockets out of sight, are a sign of an introverted or defensive nature.
- *Wide, expansive movements* – arms that are flung outwards and away from the body – are associated with someone with a more extroverted personality.
- *Gestures betraying anger and aggression* are too numerous and well-known to list, but a few choice ones include thumping a tightly clenched fist on a table, stabbing the air with the index finger or curling the fingers stiffly into a claw-like pose.

Health notes

Studies in a home for the mentally ill showed a tendency for those in the home to sit rocking themselves while holding their thumbs inside their clenched fists. Hand analysts consider the thumbs to be the most important of the digits, as they represent willpower, determination and strength of character. Hiding our thumbs is a sign of withdrawal, tantamount to saying that we don't want to know, and are either unwilling or incapable of using our willpower to change our circumstances.

Hand tremors

These come in various forms, and may indicate serious conditions. The shaky hand of the DT's (delirium tremens), following a heavily alcoholic night, should pass off the next day. But an inveterate drinker is given away by a constant fine hand tremor, which will only be cured after 'drying out'. These shakes may equally occur as a result of drug abuse or when patients swallow large doses of certain minerals – as in lead or mercury poisoning.

Degrees of tremor

With hyperthyroidism, an hormonal disorder, a fine hand tremor is one of the early symptoms, especially aggravated when the arm is extended and the fingers stretched out. Fine tremors may also indicate disorders of the central nervous system or diseases that progressively waste away the muscles. A more dramatic tremor can occur in multiple sclerosis. Here, the muscle spasms may produce a coarse shaking when the individual reaches out to touch an object, although no tremor exists when the hand is relaxed or at rest.

Tread carefully

As with all aspects of health, a definitive diagnosis should never be attempted from signs in the hands alone – certainly not from one symptom such as tremor – and not by anyone other than a qualified medical practitioner. Fine tremors are a case in point, for they can easily be confused with other conditions such as familial tremor, a harmless inherited condition that seems to occur when the individual is either emotionally aroused or particularly self-conscious.

And, of course, tremor is a recognizable symptom that accompanies states of fear, anxiety and hysteria. In these cases, the involuntary movements of the hands and fingers are nervous tremors with no rhythmic pattern, and which subside when the individual is calmed. Nervous gestures – erratic, uncontrolled or inappropriate movements of the hands when the individual is in a state of high arousal – fall into this category, too.

Hypoglycaemia (low glucose levels in the blood) can also cause tremor. Although more often associated with diabetes, it can occur more innocuously as a result of an over-strict dieting regime or going without food for long periods of time – in the latter case, a fine finger-tremble disappears when glucose or fruit juices are taken. And drinking too much strong coffee can also bring on temporary shake

Parkinson's disease

There is, however, one type of tremor that is unmistakable and is known as 'pill-rolling' – an involuntary rhythmic movement of the thumb tip rubbing against the tip of the index finger. This is a characteristic symptom of Parkinson's disease. It tends to occur when the hand is at rest, but disappears with movement.

Temperature

This often gives away health clues, but use common sense to decide whether other, temporary factors might be causing the changes (see below).

The four hand types

When considering the overall appearance of the hand, the four elemental hand types are another important factor. The following provides a summary of these types (see also Part One, pages 16–17, and 'Your line type', page 102).

The Earth hand

Practical, stable outdoor types

Earth-type susceptibilities:

- worry
- bowel or intestinal problems
- skin ailments
- problems with joints
- physical fatigue

The Air hand

Chatty communicators with a passion for learning

Air-type susceptibilities:

- headaches
- a delicate nervous system
- respiratory problems
- ear, nose and throat complaints
- colds and chills
- mental fatigue

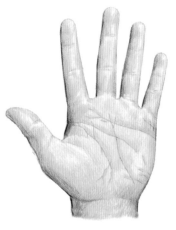

Temperature-related clues

- Hands that are too cold despite a warm ambient temperature may denote a circulatory problem.
- If the hands are cold and dry with a doughy feel to them, they could be suggesting an underactive thyroid, particularly if the fingers are podgy and sausage-like. Obesity is also another symptom here.
- Shock, from either injury or sudden emotional trauma, produces characteristic physiological symptoms that include cold, clammy hands. This is often accompanied by excessive perspiration. Mild anxiety and nervousness can also make hands cold and sweaty.
- Hot, sweaty hands (whose owner hasn't just been doing aerobics!), may be a corroborating symptom of an overactive thyroid.
- Hands that are hot and dry may be associated with hypertension or kidney problems.
- Very hot and dry hands often accompany a high fever.
- A warm, dry skin, unless otherwise dried through overuse of detergents, chemicals or solvents, could be symptomatic of nutritional deficiencies.

The Fire hand

Super-dynamo types, at home in the fast lane

Fire-type susceptibilities:

- accidents and injuries from burns and sharp objects
- cardiovascular problems
- backache and problems of the spinal column
- chills and feverishness
- mental and physical burn-out

The Water hand

Sensitive, gentle and refined romantics

Water-type susceptibilities:

- sensitive digestive system
- depression, neuroses, obsessional behaviour and similar psychological conditions
- delicate skin
- allergic reactions
- rheumatic ailments
- delicate immune system
- complications of the reproductive system
- low physical stamina and resources
- addiction

Colour

Hand colour is a very useful general clue. One of the most obvious examples here is of heavy smoking, where brown stains on the tops of the first two fingers invariably give the game away. The attendant effects to one's health from this habit are too numerous to list here, but an investigation of the smoker's hand may well reveal whether other factors exist that could potentially be aggravated by smoking. A predisposition to disorders of the respiratory tract, for example, is quite easy to spot, and if the slightest susceptibility to chronic bronchitis, coronary disease or even cancer of the lungs is suspected then the message here is quite plain.

Racial factors

While most of the information regarding health aspects in the hand is common to all nationalities, unhappily not enough research has been carried out on colour changes in black hands. But, since colour is only one of many factors to be considered, there should be enough clues elsewhere in the hand to arrive at a satisfactory conclusion across all races.

Note: Certain auto-immune disorders may also cause abnormal pigmentation of the skin on the hands. Vitiligo, for example, is a condition that produces pale patches of skin, giving the hand a blotchy appearance, while in the condition known as Addison's disease the skin takes on a darker pigmentation, as if the hand were tanned, although there has been no exposure to the sun or to artificial tanning agents.

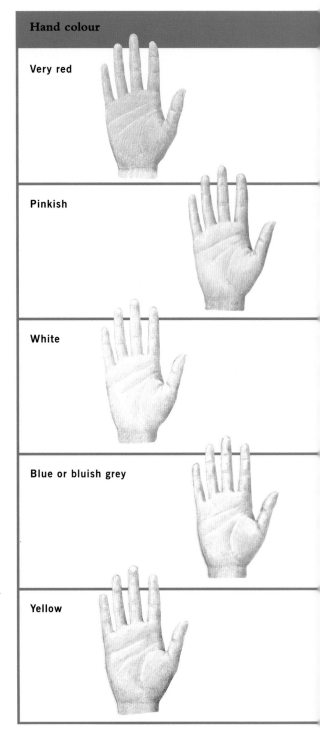

Hand colour

Very red

Pinkish

White

Blue or bluish grey

Yellow

Psychological make-up	Health pointers	
• Irascible temperament • Anger • Passion • Energy	• Possible high blood pressure • Possible liver dysfunction, especially cirrhosis of the liver • Glandular disorders • Gouty conditions • Susceptibility to stroke • Diabetes	• Feverish conditions • High temperatures • Exposure to chemicals, allergens or inclement weather • Reddish blush on percussion edge is sometimes a sign of pregnancy
• A well-balanced disposition	Whatever the race, a pinkish tinge to the hand is the sign of a healthy constitution.	
• Self-centredness • Lack of warmth towards others • Lack of energy or enthusiasm	• Possible iron-deficiency anaemia • Poor circulation • Low blood pressure • Anxiety • Shock	
• Critical • Sluggish nature • Slow to react or respond • Inactive, couch-potato type • Nervous disposition prone to shock	• Circulatory, cardiovascular or respiratory problems, especially if hand is both blue and warm (known as cyanosis, the condition can give a blue tinge to the nail bed, nails and eventually the fingers and palms)	• Shock (blueness accompanied by a cold and clammy feel) • Adverse reactions to chemicals or drugs • Effects from severe cold
• A jaundiced point of view • Envious • Resentful • Gloomy outlook • Depressed	• Jaundice • Severe cases of pernicious anaemia • Hepatitis • An excess of betacarotene (from eating a huge quantity of carrots or drinking too much carrot juice)	If none of these conditions are corroborated, a yellow tinting of the skin can sometimes point to a very high cholesterol count, thus putting the cardiovascular system in jeopardy.

Indications in the Nails

Reading the shapes and signs

Two major things for any hand analyst to consider are nail shape and any 'irregularities'.

The square nail
• Parallel sides and a straight base.
• Hale and hearty, stable, equanimical person who is slow to anger.
• The longer, more rectangular, variation also reflects an even-tempered individual, but with a certain fussiness that may include hypochondria.
• A very short square nail reflects a nervous, critical, irritable nature, prone to selfishness, emotional affectation and neurosis and lacking warmth towards others.

The long, narrow nail
• A rounded base and narrow enough to display a good deal of digit either side of the nail.
• A full set of long, narrow nails suggests emotional instability, often with a tendency towards repression and psychological disorders.
• Physiologically, these people are generally rather delicate, but with a great deal of nervous energy.
• Extremely narrow nails highlight hypersensitivity.
• Nails that are narrow and thick, tending to curve into a talon shape, suggest dietary deficiencies and poor elimination of toxins.

The fan-shaped nail
• Triangular shape where the nail tapers to a point at its root.
• A very sensitive, often impulsive disposition; possibly irrational or neurotic.
• Physiologically, nails may adopt this shape as a result of severe stress or emotional shock, but the fan shape is generally an important warning sign that stress is one of the owner's weak links.

The wide nail
• Parallel sides and a straight base, but much broader in comparison to its height.
• Reflects an explosive temper that, once it has subsided, leaves no lasting sulkiness.
• Physiologically, these types are considered strong and resilient, although some hand analysts describe this as an apoplectic type.

Health notes

Vitamins A and D are believed to be helpful in maintaining healthy nails, as is Silica amongst the tissue salts, as well as Combination K.

Nail irregularities

Any deformities of the horny nail itself point to damage of the growth process – and therefore to physiological irregularities. Also nails may be affected by the weather: extreme damp can cause distortion, and nails break more in winter.

▲ Horizontal ridging

• These grooves confirm the nail's growth rate and also coincide with physical or psychological trauma, showing that catastrophic events disrupt the smooth flow of the keratinous material that makes up the nail.

• A single horizontal ridge across one nail probably results from damage to that nail itself.

• A horizontal ridge on all the nails can show some injury or trauma to the system – a crash diet or an emotional shock, say. In the latter case, the ridge forms at the nail's root, or growing point, and works upwards as the nail grows out. As a nail takes about six months to grow from root to tip, the date of a trauma can be estimated. A horizontal groove halfway up your nail, for example, suggests that it was roughly three months ago.

▲ Vertical ridging

• Heavy vertical ridging tends to occur with age but can also be associated with a delicate, allergen-sensitive physiology. In many cases, the ridging is considered to be hereditary and highlights inherited health susceptibilities.

• Rheumatoid arthritis is especially linked to a full set of nails with heavy vertical ridges. As with all diseases represented by discoloration or irregularities of the nails, once recovery takes place the nails return to normal.

▲ The concave

• A full set of dished nails suggests a lack of energy. Constant exposure to chemicals, water or softeners such as oils may swell and soften the nails

Other ridging indications

Problems associated with horizontal ridging:

• A sudden interruption to the blood supply – a heart attack, say – can interfere with nail production

• Infectious diseases such as mumps, measles and scarlet fever, acute infections and high fevers

• If all the nails show a series of horizontal ridges, this represents a longer period of disturbance to the system

• Poor nutrition, possibly due to severe dieting, and also deficiencies of vitamins A, B-complex and D

• Broken bones

• Long-term stress

Problems associated with vertical ridging:

• An overactive thyroid gland

• Some chronic skin diseases

• Gastric disorders

▲ The convex nail

• This often points to respiratory problems, including persistent colds, coughs and bronchitis, and may be found in the hands of smokers. The curving so that they grow curved.

• Occasionally, the condition is found with certain mental illnesses.

• Physiologically (and fairly commonly), this is a sign of nutritional deficiencies, specifically a serious mineral imbalance that weakens and thins the nail. Recovery follows starts with the nail on the left index finger, followed by the right index, the left middle finger then the right middle finger.

• Progressive weakening of the lungs is reflected by all ten nails being hooked.

• If smoking is stopped, the nails return to normal.

improved diet together with vitamin, mineral or tissue-salt supplements.

• The concave nail is also linked to iron-deficiency anaemia. Quite common among childbearing and pre-menopausal women, the nails normally return to normal when iron supplements are taken.

Nail colour

In the ideal hand, the colour of the nail bed should match the pigmentation of the palm, so that in the European hand the nail has a healthy pinkish tinge to it, while in the African hand the nail tends to be pinky-beige. Smooth, transparent and with a satiny sheen, the nail should be gently rounded from side to side and slightly springy from top to bottom. Moons should be well defined and milky-white.

- Too pallid can indicate iron-deficiency anaemia. Low vitality is associated with pale-pink nails.
- White, and even yellow, coloration can point to liver dysfunction. Certain venereal diseases, too, are associated with whitish-yellow nails.
- Cyanosis (the bluish skin coloration caused by circulatory troubles) also leaves its characteristic blue tinge within the nail bed.
- Yellow nails can suggest jaundice and other problems affecting the liver. Too much betacarotene will also leave a distinctive yellow tinge on the nail beds.
- Very red nails suggest high blood pressure and a tendency towards cardiovascular disease.

Harmful invaders

The nail itself may also come under attack, mainly from bacterial or fungal infection. A common one is Paronychia, a condition that causes the nail bed, cuticle and surrounding fingertip to swell and become very sore. If not treated, this can cause thickening, severe ridging, discoloration and eventual distortion.

▲ The humped nail
- Sometimes called the Hippocratic nail (after the ancient Greek medical scholar Hippocrates, who first described it and associated it with such lung diseases as pneumonia and tuberculosis), it is still recognized today as a symptom of certain respiratory disorders.
- A predisposition to cardiovascular problems, emphysema, heart disease and poor oxygenation is suggested.
- It can be symptomatic of cirrhosis of the liver. Some severe cases also feature clubbed fingers (fingers with distorted bulbous tips). With other signs, such as cyanosis (blue discoloration), these can indicate lung tumours.
- Humped nails return to normal after treatment.

Pitting and thickening
- Tiny indentations and roughness may suggest psoriasis. Severe psoriasis may make the nails thicken and detach themselves from the nail bed.
- Diseases affecting the auto-immune system might be implicated by severe pitting.
- If the nails thicken and toughen noticeably, becoming hard to cut, and especially if they take on a yellow hue, it may implicate lymphatic problems, cardiovascular disease or diabetes.

Brittle nails
- Thin, flaky or brittle nails can signal mineral imbalance.
- A lack of calcium and protein may be responsible for weak, soft nails (as may the cold and damp).
- Brittle, slow-growing, lacklustre nails may be associated with an underactive thyroid gland.

Moon colour and form

- Ideally, the moons (often only visible on the thumbs) should be milky white in colour.
- Moons that are tinged with blue denote respiratory disorders and possible cardiovascular problems.
- Over-large moons suggest a predisposition to an overactive thyroid.
- No moons may suggest an underactive thyroid gland; also generally linked to a weaker constitution.
- Poorly formed moons may point to a predisposition to heart disease.

Spots and speckling

Apart from uniform discoloration of the nail bed, a variety of coloured speckling may also occur.

▲ **White spots or specks**
These have long been considered a sign of calcium deficiency, in particular that of calcium phosphate. This may indeed be the case but, as many people with these markings have not found an improvement when augmenting their intake of calcium-rich foods, it would suggest that perhaps another agent is either deficient or at fault, and is impeding adequate uptake of the mineral. Current thinking lays the blame on a deficiency of zinc, magnesium and, possibly, the vitamin B6.

On the psychological side, tiredness and anxiety can produce these characteristic speckled marks, too. Interestingly, the speckling disappears as the stress levels are reduced and the problems resolved.

▲ **Horizontal white lines**
White lines that occur in the nail but that do not cause the fabric of the nail itself to form into ridges (as in Beau's lines) are known as Mee's lines. While in some cases these lines denote nutritional deficiencies, they are more widely documented as reflecting poisoning from certain minerals, such as arsenic and thallium. They are particularly associated with acute fever and are also implicated in certain coronary diseases.

▲ **Black specks**
One of the symptoms of bacterial infection of the heart valves is recognized as tiny bruises that show up in the form of long, thin black specks underneath the nail.

▲ **Red streaks**
Similar streaks to the black ones, but this time red in colour, are associated with long-term high blood pressure. Bacterial infection of the heart may be implicated in severe cases.

▲ **Pale nail bed**
When the nail bed is pale in colour, with a thin red band appearing towards the top (near the free edge of the nail), liver disease may be suspected.

▲ **Fawn-white coloration**
A nail where the bottom half is a brownish-fawn colour while the top half remains white, is associated with kidney disease.

Indications in Skin Patterns

Reading the ridges

The papillary ridge patterns of the fingertips give us a starting point for personality profiles and so also hint at which health problems may occur.

The loop

A majority of loop patterns in the fingertips is the sign of a cooperative nature and an easy-going disposition. These people enjoy masses of different interests. Quick to react, they love the adrenalin-surge that goes with a busy, buzzing life, filled with variety.

Health indications:
Susceptibility to nervous problems, such as nervous fatigue and even mental breakdown, may be suspected.

The whorl

A majority of whorl patterns is the mark of intensity. Such people are deep thinkers, slow to react and extremely individualistic in their outlook. These are people who tend to keep their feelings to themselves.

Health indications:
Can be inner tension leading to either intestinal, digestive or cardiovascular problems. Owners of whorls would do well to practise deep breathing relaxation techniques regularly.

The arch

A majority of arch patterns normally denotes a practical, hard-working and down-to-earth individual. These people can possess a certain reserve that hinders their ability to express their innermost feelings.

Health indications:
The tendency to bottle up emotions can lead to ulcers and digestive disorders, on the physical side, and on the psychological side, may point to anxieties linked with repression and even to a nervous breakdown. There may also be a predisposition to hypertension, and inherited heart problems are associated with the arch pattern. Any form of creative pursuit that allows free expression of the imagination is excellent cathartic therapy for arched types. Any creative aptitude should be encouraged from a very young age.

Tented arch

Tented arches tend to suggest highly strung, sensitive individuals.

Health indications:

Nervous problems may be indicated here, and impulsiveness – which is a characteristic of this type – could well result in accidents and injury.

Composite

Composite patterns show an inability to make up one's mind, and a mentality that needs to see all sides of the picture before reaching a conclusion.

Health indications:

Mental fatigue can result from over-speculation and excessive brooding.

Scientific evidence

During the early 1900s, much scientific attention was focused on skin-ridge patterns in an attempt to determine whether mental or physiological abnormalities imprint themselves in our palms and fingertips. The giants amongst these pioneers were Harold Cummins, Charles Midlo and L.S. Penrose. Charlotte Wolff, a psychologist, also carried out a great deal of research amongst patients with learning disorders. Evidence was found to confirm that abnormal patterns highlight a predisposition to certain types of mental illness. Further, it was shown that particular patterns may also point to various congenital and psychological disorders such as heart disease and obsessive behaviour.

Triradii patterns

These skin patterns – occurring where three sets of ridges meet – play an important part in medical investigation. In dermatoglyphic studies, particular attention is focused on three triradii. The first two are located on the palm just beneath the index and little finger and are named respectively 'a' and 'd'. The third, or axial triradius, which in the normal hand lies at the base of the palm, is known as 't'. When lines are drawn down from the two top triradii to join the third at the base of the palm, the angle formed is known as the 'atd' angle. In a normal hand, this angle should measure roughly 45 degrees. If the angle is much wider, due to the basal triradius occurring higher up the palm, studies suggest that a heart defect may exist requiring further investigation.

— · — · — · —	normal
— · — · — · —	possible health problems

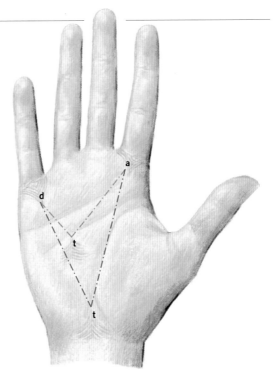

Down's syndrome

Of all the research carried out in this field, the most widely recognized are the findings concerning Down's syndrome, a condition caused directly by chromosomal abnormalities. While irregularities of the major lines tend to occur with this syndrome, several features of the skin ridges, depending on the gravity of the condition, may also appear. For example, the ridges tend to flow in a more horizontal direction across the palm due to the displacement further up in the hand of the axial triradius – the 'atd' angle being greater than 45 degrees (see previous page). There is also a higher incidence of ulna loops on the fingertips and a greater likelihood of complex patterns occurring on the Luna mount, while a decrease of patterns in the Venus area has been observed.

The Simian line (see page 81) across the palm and the higher axial triradius are indicators of Down's syndrome.

Passing it on

Scientific studies have shown that either one or both parents of Down's syndrome children possess unusual ridge patterns, even though they do not themselves show outward symptoms of Down's, suggesting some fault in their genes that could be transmitted to their offspring. Here, in particular, when it comes to genetic counselling, knowledge of ridging could prove invaluable.

Health notes

Although a wealth of research confirms that almost all individuals with chromosomal abnormalities possess unusual ridge patterns, different disorders do not mark the hands in specific ways. In short, it is not necessarily possible to distinguish one disorder from another simply by looking at the ridging.

Other indications

Doctors in India have linked misaligned axial triradii with congenital heart disease. This confirms earlier research carried out among Japanese-Hawaiians, which found that sixty-four per cent of male patients with congenital heart disease also possessed a triradius that was displaced halfway up the palm, in comparison to seventeen per cent in the control group.

Much research has also been carried out on the dermal patterns of subjects with schizophrenia. Certainly, unusual patterns do occur, which could point to genetic defects, but none of the studies has been able to identify distinctive patterns that are characteristic to this disease alone.

Although the patterns laid down at birth never change, interruptions in the skin ridges –

The 'string of pearls' effect

called the 'string of pearls' effect – may occur through ill-health and dietary deficiency, often when the body is out of sync and its defences are vulnerable. Fittingly, AIDS patients have been found to display this effect. The 'pearls' feature is also implicated in mental illness, and seems to crop up among people who are suffering from schizophrenia or milder mental disturbance such as neurosis. When health is back to normal, the ridges normally reunite.

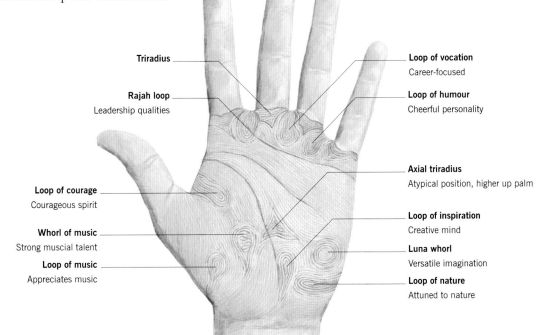

Triradius

Rajah loop
Leadership qualities

Loop of vocation
Career-focused

Loop of humour
Cheerful personality

Axial triradius
Atypical position, higher up palm

Loop of courage
Courageous spirit

Whorl of music
Strong muscial talent

Loop of music
Appreciates music

Loop of inspiration
Creative mind

Luna whorl
Versatile imagination

Loop of nature
Attuned to nature

Typical and atypical hands

	Fingerprints	Ridge count	Palm patterns	'atd' angle
The typical hand	The most common fingerprint pattern is the loop, closely followed by the whorl. Arches occur less commonly. It is usual to find a mixture of fingerprint patterns.	The normal ridge count of a loop is 12–14.	On the palm itself it is more usual to find an open-field arrangement of ridges – where the ridges flow with no specific patterning. Complex patterns such as the whorl are less common.	The normal 'atd' angle is 45 degrees.
The atypical hand	Arches and ulna loops are more common. In general, the same pattern occurs on all ten digits.	On average, there is a lower ridge count.	More complex patterns of whorls, loops and composites tend to recur on the palm.	Because the axial triradius is displaced higher up in the palm, the 'atd' angle is often greater than 45 degrees.

Indications in the Mounts and Plains

Top of the palm

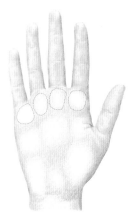

Think of the mounts and plains as a fascinating landscape – one that can reveal all manner of indications as to psychological and physical health. Remember: a dominant mount indicates your salient characteristics, while a mount that is particularly large or small suggests an over-abundance or lack of the associated qualities. Alternatively, you may find that you have two equally dominant mounts, in which case the qualities of both are combined.

Mount of Jupiter

Physical characteristics
Jupiterian types are often well-built and usually enjoy a robust, vigorous constitution.

Psychological profile
Warm and friendly, social and generous (though sometimes with a tendency to extravagance) – these are the hallmarks of the Jupiterian. If your mount is dominant, it is a sign that you are lively and noisy, and you will often seem able to fill a house all on your own.

When well-proportioned
This shows a well-balanced, stable character, able to take things in their stride.

When over-developed
These are larger-than-life characters whose vast appetites could well prove to be the downfall of their health. This is especially the case when the mount is not only over-developed but also appears to be very red in colour.

> ### Health notes
>
> Characterized by a huge appetite, Jupiterians love rich food and good wine and, unless there are signs of restraint elsewhere in their hands, consume plenty of both throughout their lifetime!

When thin and flat
This may indicate depression.

Predisposition to ill-health
Because of their huge appetites and penchant for high living, most Jupiterians have a tendency to put on weight unless they watch their diets. Bronchial problems, intestinal complaints, hypertension and strokes are all diseases associated with the Jupiterian. Lines formed into long islands that lie across this mount may well confirm a vulnerability to chest infections, coughs and colds.

Mount of Saturn

Physical characteristics
Often tall and thin with a prominent bone structure, Saturnians may generally be described as wiry types, lean and sinewy.

Psychological profile
Typically serious, quiet, sensible types with plenty of self-control, who are readily able to shoulder responsibility. The negative side of the Saturnian produces introversion, lugubriousness and a fatalistic or even morbid outlook.

When well-proportioned
Best for this mount to be slightly on the flat side, neither over- nor under-developed. In comparison to its neighbours, the Saturn mount should always appear lower and flatter – such a mount denotes good physical and mental health.

When over-developed
Of all the mounts, this one should not be overly developed because, when it is, it denotes a morose

> ## Health notes
>
> Those with over-developed Saturn mounts find it difficult to express affection for others and, because they are such critical nit-pickers, may find others just as reluctant to give affection back!

individual, an introverted loner and misanthropist with strong tendencies to paranoia, moodiness and depression.

When thin and flat
General constitutional weaknesses, often with a sense of irresponsibility and a need for escapism.

Predisposition to ill-health
Saturnians tend to lack vitality. Their teeth may be a source of trouble and, though many are musical, hearing problems are characteristic. They are prone to biliousness, nervous complaints, rheumatic ailments in particular, liver problems, varicose veins and haemorrhoids.

Mount of Apollo

Physical characteristics
Typical Apollonians are of average stature but their bodies are graceful and agile, with figures that might be described as athletic. As a rule they are very healthy types, undoubtedly due to their invariably happy and positive attitude to life.

Psychological profile
Positive, happy people with a lively and buoyant disposition. Usually well-balanced emotionally.

When well-proportioned
This indicates a sunny disposition.

When over-developed
Extravagance, exhibitionism and vanity are predominant.

When thin and flat
Dull and emotionally repressed, these people have particular difficulty in communicating with others. Timidity and introversion will often hold them back in life. Heart trouble is one of the physiological weak links.

Predisposition to ill-health
The cheerfully positive attitude of the Apollonian character seems to keep many maladies at bay. They are, however, prone to feverish conditions, problems with sight and cardiovascular diseases.

Mount of Mercury

Physical characteristics

People with dominant Mercury mounts invariably have a Peter Pan quality that keeps them looking much younger than their years. Of small to medium stature, but well-proportioned, their most telling characteristics are quick, nervous, almost bird-like gestures; their animated faces and alert eyes don't seem to miss a trick. In general, Mercurians enjoy fairly good health.

Psychological profile

The ability to communicate with others is represented by this mount.

When well-proportioned

A well-padded and well-developed mount of Mercury suggests a warm, receptive, socially well-balanced disposition, someone who is interested in others and in the affairs of the world and finds it easy to integrate and communicate.

Health notes

Because of their craving for constant excitement, those with overly large Mercury mounts may be drawn to stimulants such as drugs or alcohol.

When over-developed

Disproportionately large Mercury mounts tend to suggest the sort who live life in the fast lane and are prone to burn-out and nervous exhaustion.

When thin and flat

Apathy is suggested here – a general lack of interest in other people and an inability to express oneself, whether verbally, emotionally or sexually. Speech defects such as a lisp sometimes occur.

Predisposition to ill-health

Nervous tension and stress are by far the biggest problems, along with intestinal or liver problems directly caused by anxiety.

Mount markings

Particular markings (crosses, squares, triangles, stars and grilles) may be found on the mounts, each influencing that mount's qualities in a positive or negative way. For example:

A cross on the Jupiter mount represents a fulfilling long-term relationship.

A square on the Saturn mount protects against adversity.

A triangle on the Apollo mount symbolizes success governed by good judgement.

A star on the Mercury mount heralds success in financial or scientific fields.

Middle and base of the palm

If the palm looks broader in the middle, or if this central band appears better developed than the top and basal parts, you are well equipped for handling physically or psychologically stressful situations. Too broad, however, especially on a very firm hand, can suggest aggressive tendencies. Conversely, if this central band of your palm appears thin, narrow and poorly developed, heavily overhung by the mounts beneath your fingers and noticeably overshadowed by the mounts at your wrist, you can suffer from a lack of resistance to stress and possess little staying power – a tranquil, harmonious working and living environment is essential to your health and well-being. Negatively, you might lack moral fibre at times, being too impressionable and easily distracted from your goals.

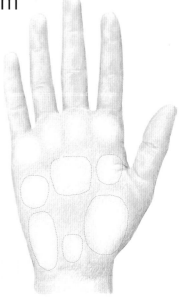

Mount of Mars Positive

Physical characteristics
Generally of medium height, Martians tend to be strongly built, solid types, often with powerful physiques. Healthwise, they enjoy a robust constitution and have plenty of get-up-and-go.

Health notes

Owners of over-developed Mars Positive mounts should learn to release their energies on a sports field, perhaps, or at the gym.

Psychological profile
Courage, energy and fighting spirit, together with a sense of self-preservation and the ability to take charge of situations.

When well-proportioned
A courageous and healthy fighting spirit, whose owner is able to balance the principles of fight and flight.

When over-developed
A disproportionately large development here suggests bottled-up aggression. Unless tempered by other factors, it can signal a dangerous personality – this is the sign of the bully, of brawn before brains. Owners of such developments seem to possess more physical energy than they know what to do with.

When thin and flat
Owners of a deficient mount tend towards a lack of positive drive, a tendency to be easily discouraged and an inability to take control of their lives. These people easily tire themselves out and are not good with stress.

Predisposition to ill-health
Feverishness, intestinal activity and bronchial conditions are associated with the Mars area. And, because of the Martian hot temper, cardiac problems are a weak link.

Mount of Mars Negative

Physical characteristics
Again, similar in stature to the other two types ruled by Mars – energetic and robust.

Psychological profile
Self-control, moral resistance, staying power and the ability to cope when under pressure are indicated by this mount.

When well-proportioned
Noticeable persistence and moral fortitude are suggested. When the mount appears harmoniously balanced with the rest, it denotes good moral fibre and also integrity.

When over-developed
A disproportionately large mount here shows an individual who stands firm when it comes to their beliefs, and cannot be swayed once they have made up their mind, even when presented with very convincing evidence to the contrary – a truly 'bloody-minded' individual!

When thin and flat
A marked lack of resistance and moral fibre.

Predisposition to ill-health
Similar indications and predispositions to the previous two categories (feverishness, plus intestinal, bronchial and cardiac conditions).

Plain of Mars

Physical characteristics
As with the other Mars areas – a well-built, strong and energetic individual.

Psychological profile
A streetwise individual with self-control over their passions and emotions.

When well-proportioned
This denotes good powers of self-control, particularly over one's emotions, aggression and reactions to life in general.

When over-developed
This suggests someone quick to flare up into a temper, sometimes uncontrollable rage. Drunkenness and lasciviousness may also be indicated.

When thin and flat
Poorly padded, so that the central palm appears thin and hollow, suggests a tendency to overreact, especially

Thick or thin?
To distinguish between a thin or a well-padded plain of Mars, hold the palm between your thumb and fingers. If the tendons in the centre (on the palm side) feel exposed and stringy, the area is thin. If they can't be felt, this area can be considered well-padded.

if this area is covered in fine, extraneous lines. Lack of development spotlights a weak character, someone with little charisma who doesn't possess the necessary stuffing to make a success out of life.

Predisposition to ill-health
Similar indications as for other Mars features (feverishness, digestive, intestinal, bronchial and cardiac problems).

Mount of Venus

Physical characteristics

Because this area covers the radial artery as it enters the palm from the wrist, as well as the muscles controlling movement of the thumb, the amount of padding and the quality of this mount give information about your resilience and vitality – both psychological and physical. Your instinctive affection and sexuality are also denoted by this mount. Venusians are characterized by their happy, friendly and optimistic attitudes to life.

Psychological profile

Expect a strong degree of sexiness, a warmth of character and a magnetic personality if the mount is well-developed, and firm but springy to the touch. A tough cookie who holds everything in, if the mount is hard. Whereas softness here shows a receptive and sympathetic nature, a flabby consistency denotes someone who is lazy and self-centred.

When well-proportioned

Joie de vivre, loving, outgoing and exuberant are characteristic descriptions here. Physically, these people tend to be energetic and robust, with the ability to simply shake off ill-health, whether physical or mental. A good libido accompanies this type of mount.

When over-developed

An excessively or disproportionately large mount denotes a hot-tempered, aggressive individual. The basic animal instincts prevail when this mount is developed to excess – a huge appetite for personal and sexual gratification together with a need for over-stimulation of the senses.

When thin and flat

Mean, narrow-minded and selfish describes this character. There is a marked lack of energy and vitality, an underactive metabolism being a possible cause. There could well be emotional difficulties,

Health notes

In some cases, sadistic tendencies might be expected with an over-developed Venus mount, especially if the rest of the palm feels hard as a board.

accompanied by a poor sex drive. Here the problems could be physical, psychological or both.

Predisposition to ill-health

Apart from a predisposition to sexually transmitted diseases amongst the more promiscuous of the sign, no particular tendencies are associated with Venusians. But it is fair to say that the fuller and better constructed the mount, the greater the vitality and resistance to disease. If the area is unduly pale, or if it throws up an angry red colour, an imbalance of the metabolic processes may be suspected.

Testing for life

To test for vitality, press the tip of your thumb into the Venus mount and, on releasing it, notice how the padding responds to the pressure. If it readily springs back, your health and recuperative powers are good; if the mount is very flabby and retains the indentation, your health may be under par and your resistance poor. If the mount is so hard that you are unable to dent the surface at all, you are likely to possess a constitution of iron.

Mount of Luna

Physical characteristics
Constitutionally, Lunarians are not very strong and may generally be prone to ill-health.

Psychological profile
The Luna mount represents your sensitivity and intuition. However, the dreamy and romantic Luna influence may at times develop into sentimentality and moodiness. Imagination, creativity and artistic ability is associated with this area. Sometimes, when this mount is over-developed, the imagination runs wild, leading to mood swings, depression and hyperanxiety. Restlessness, coupled with mental and physical instability, which is mainly due to unrealistic expectations and living with one's head in the clouds, is also represented here.

When well-proportioned
A sign of a sensitive, imaginative and creative mentality.

When over-developed
This may imply an over-impressionable nature, a 'Walter Mitty' person who believes their own delusions. Renal, bladder and rheumatic disorders in particular are associated with an over-large Luna mount, as are neurosis, insanity and other mental problems.

Moon and mental health

The words 'lunacy' and 'lunatic' are derived from the Latin word *luna* ('moon'), as it was believed that the effect of the Moon could bring about madness. Interestingly, an excessively emphasized Luna mount in the bottom of the palm of the hand is indeed associated with a personality that has a predisposition to mental instability.

When thin and flat
When it is poorly developed, or even missing altogether, it is the sign of the true hypochondriac.

Predisposition to ill-health
Lunarians are prone to a wide range of problems, including melancholia, moodiness, anxiety, restlessness and all manner of psychological disorders, especially if the mount is covered with numerous fine lines. Rheumatic ailments, problems of the bowels and large intestine, and gynaecological/urological problems are all associated with this type. So too are alcohol dependency (especially if the area is very red) and drug addiction (emphasized by very white mounts). Lunarians are particularly vulnerable to alcohol and drugs, as these provide escapism from the harsh realities of life.

Mount of Neptune

The mount of Neptune connects the physical side of the palm (which is represented by the mount of Venus) with the subconscious side (symbolized by the mount of Luna), and acts as a bridge that carries and processes information between the two. In terms of health, comparatively little is known about this area, although research on it continues. However, early evidence suggests that a well-developed mount here – and especially one that is marked with the basal triradius – could be a sign of the sensitive healer, and especially of those who are drawn to any therapies requiring 'hands-on' techniques (such as chiropractors or reflexologists, for example).

Mount markings

As introduced on page 62, certain markings may be found on the mounts, and these can influence the qualities of the mount in question (either negatively or positively). Here are some examples for the mounts (and plain) found in the middle and base of the palm.

A triangle on Mars Positive represents the ability to make valuable use of one's own strength and courage.

A cross on Mars Negative is unfavourable and indicates antagonistic influences.

A cross on the plain of Mars symbolizes an interest in complementary health techniques and esoteric topics.

A grille on the mount of Venus indicates extremely heightened emotions.

A star on the mount of Luna is cautionary, and indicates potential danger during travel.

Indications in the Major Lines

The Life line

Each major line covers a different aspect of well-being, so where better to start than with the Life line, fount of vitality? But remember: although this line (as with all other major lines in the hand) will contain certain clues about the individual's state of health, the markings represent *only* a predisposition, not an inevitability.

Psychological indications

A Life line that is widely separated from the Head line at its start suggests a reckless, impulsive nature and a tendency to accidents and injuries. But one that is joined to the Head line for some distance denotes sensitivity and reticence, perhaps a shyness or lack of self-confidence that may impede emotional and intellectual development, sometimes even blighting that individual's chances of leading a truly independent life. As for the Life line that begins on the Mars mount, close to the base of the thumb, and then arches upwards before regaining its sweep around the ball of the thumb, hot-headedness and temper tantrums might be expected here.

Physiological indications

The strength of the line corresponds to the strength of our physical constitution. So, with a faint, poorly formed line, interrupted by islands and breaks, suspect poor vitality, a weakened constitution and a susceptibility to ill-health. A line that is uneven throughout its length – sometimes strong and deep, at other times thin and weak – denotes patchy health. This is a warning that you must pace yourself better –

taking on too much during your 'strong' periods is leading to your weaker patches.

The line's journey around the ball of the thumb is also very telling. A wide sweep where the line arcs its way to the centre of the palm means that it encircles an ample mount of Venus. As this mount represents an energy store, such a formation indicates good resistance and

_____ Life	_____ Head

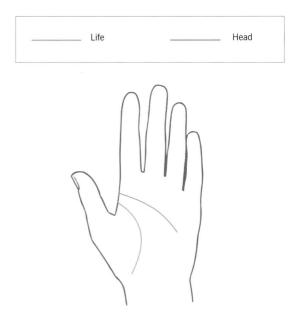

Life line widely separated from Head line

excellent powers of recuperation. Conversely, if the line follows the root of the thumb closely, it means that the Venus mount is meagre and general health poor. The latter also suggests a limited sex drive, perhaps with conception problems and, in extreme cases, possible frigidity or impotence.

Length

Much worry has centred around the length of the Life line, as a short one has been mistakenly reputed to indicate a short life. The length of our Life lines do not correspond to the length of our lives – indeed, many elderly people have been found to possess short Life lines, and vice versa. (See also box opposite.)

Long or short

Very few true short Life lines exist because, when examined closely, most apparently short lines are found to be connected by a fine hairline to a new section of Life line, either further out towards the centre of the palm or overlapping another on the inside, situated closer towards the thumb. So most 'short' lines are in fact broken ones. Psychologically, a broken Life line denotes some change; physiologically, it might denote a serious health problem. But remember that lines change. Some babies possess short Life lines that then grow as the child matures, often becoming stronger, too, and shedding any other negative markings they may have.

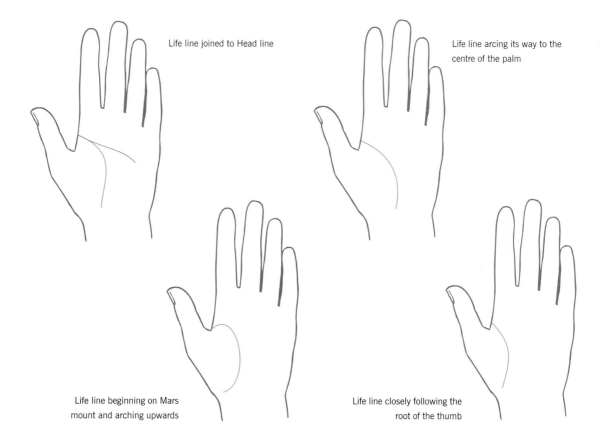

Life line joined to Head line

Life line arcing its way to the centre of the palm

Life line beginning on Mars mount and arching upwards

Life line closely following the root of the thumb

Markings in the Life line

Any markings relating to health in the Life line can be timed (see pages 88–9) with a good degree of accuracy so that, if detected early enough, preventive action may be taken. See pages 74–5 for general notes about the different markings.

Islands

Frequently found in the Life line, the presence of islands there denotes a splitting of energy and so a weakening of the constitution. A series of islands, or chain, shows a continued undermining of our general health. A fine tracery of links that breaks up the line halfway around its course may be linked to a deficiency of zinc.

Breaks

Breaks in the Life line need to be investigated carefully. If discovered early enough, and if appropriate action is taken, the line may mend itself before there is any real health danger.

There is a great difference between finding a broken line in the dominant hand as opposed

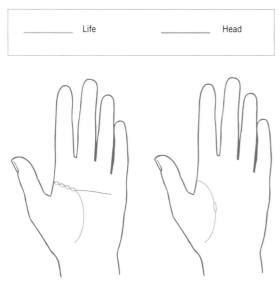

| Life | Head |

Island at the top
Many Life lines are joined at their start with the Head line: where they intertwine they may form a 'chain-effect' series of islands. This first section of the line represents our early years, so the chain may suggest childhood problems (like illness or unhappiness at school). These implications may have repercussions elsewhere in the hand or even affect our adult lives. A predisposition to respiratory problems such as asthma and sinusitis is another possibility.

Island halfway down
Occurring lower down the line, an island is associated with back problems.

Island towards the bottom
This may represent the general 'run-down' state that often leads to the common diseases of middle age. Urological or gynaecological problems may be depicted, as well as illnesses affecting the alimentary canal, the cardiovascular system and other problems linked with this age group.

Island at the base
There is speculation that a tiny, well-formed, oval-shaped island on the Life line at the base of the palm may imply a predisposition to cancer. This theory, however, requires a great deal more research. Remembering that an island reflects a weakened constitution, that a position so far along the line represents older age, and that cancer is more prevalent among the elderly, it can be seen how this correlation could be made.

to the passive one. In the passive hand, a break may denote the possibility of a major problem; in the dominant hand, it greatly increases the risk of a serious accident or health breakdown. Where both hands possess the same broken line, the odds are stacked in favour of a health breakdown – take preventative steps as soon as you can.

Horizontal crossing lines

Lines that cut horizontally across the Life line are known as trauma lines and denote a time of stress or emotional upheaval. The stronger, deeper and longer the line, the greater the effects. Shorter, shallower crossing lines suggest that the interference is temporary and, given that no adverse markings follow on the main line, there should be no long-term negative effects. A series of closely-packed fine lines should not be confused with trauma lines as the former denote a generally highly-strung disposition rather than indicating an isolated traumatic event.

Overlapping line

A seemingly short Life line may be overlapped by a new section of line with, very often, a fine hairline thread connecting the two. Overlapped lines are not as serious as clean breaks, but nevertheless denote a break in continuity and a major change in your life. Other markings in the hand will throw light on whether the change is psychological or physiological.

What is important in these cases is to note the condition and position of the new section of line. If it is strong and well-formed, you are likely to adapt well to your new circumstances and may even find your new life better than the old. But if the line is further islanded, or bears other negative markings, it could indicate that your new life will not be without difficulties and may have some detrimental effects on your health.

New or restricted horizons?

As for position, if the new section develops on the outside, sweeping its way towards the centre of the palm, it denotes a more active, expansive life. But, should the new section lie inside the old – that is, on the thumb side – the new life may bring restrictions. If all other indications in the hand suggest that the break is a psychological one, the restriction may be something like limited finances.

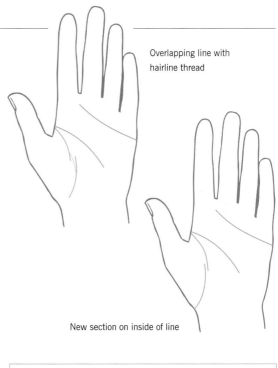

Overlapping line with hairline thread

New section on inside of line

| _____ | Life | _____ | Heart |
| _____ | Head | | |

If a physical upheaval is suggested, such as a serious accident, limitation of physical activity may be highlighted – developing agoraphobia, perhaps, or experiencing problems with the use of a limb.

Any consequences of the disturbance may be echoed by corresponding markings in the other main lines, and also by the condition of the Life line immediately beneath the point where the trauma line crosses. An island in the line, for example, suggests that the event may unsettle the individual's health for some time, while a star denotes a shock of some kind. Trauma lines can be measured and timed against the Life line at the point where they cross. This could well give the individual enough warning to avert the situation.

▶ New section

Sometimes what appears to be a break might simply be the development of a new section of line, leading further out towards the centre of the palm. In this case, the marking suggests the beginning of a whole new way of life and wider horizons.

a Horizontal trauma lines

These crossing lines may sometimes also cut through the Fate, Head and Heart lines, emphasizing their indications. Trauma lines that denote an intense period of tension can often be made to disappear by taking a more relaxed view of life, reviewing diet, and so on.

b/c The cross

Some hand analysts see this marking, together with its sister formation, the star, as a warning of impending illness that will require hospitalization, possibly even surgery.

d Dots

A sign of physical trauma. If the dot appears markedly red or blue, it could highlight the possibility of circulatory problems at the age indicated on the line (this coloration also applies to the nails, skin or the lines).

e Fraying

Don't confuse these fraying lines (which denote draining energy) with stronger single dropping branches (which indicate movement and travel).

◀ True break

A real break, one that could be a warning of injury or a life-threatening disease, is where an actual gap occurs in the line.

_____ Life		_____ Heart	
_____ Head			

Protective markings

When any negative mark occurs in the Life line, always examine the line carefully for mitigating factors. One such is a square formation, composed of four tiny lines, lying directly over the break. This is a sign of protection, implying that, despite the gravity of the situation, the subject should make a full recovery.

Another protective marking is the line of Mars. This is a line of varied length, found on the inside (thumb side) of the Life line and running parallel to it. Throughout its duration it represents a boost to vitality, so that if it occurs alongside a break in the Life line, or any other negative marking, it bolsters up the weakened constitution. Think of it as a reserve parachute – just in case.

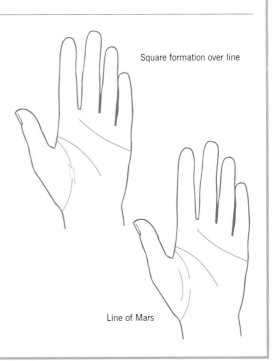

Square formation over line

Line of Mars

Cross

Two short bars forming a cross over the main Life line is said to denote a time of physical danger, when energy reserves are being dangerously depleted.

Fraying

A fraying main Life line suggests a draining of energy and lowering of resistance to disease.

Dots and indentations

A tiny indentation or dot in the line is said to represent a temporary shock to the body. An illness that responds quickly to treatment may be represented in this way but a series of these indentations, looking like a row of pin-pricks, may suggest that the nerves in the back and the spinal cord are under strain.

Health notes

A diamond- or triangular-shaped group of lines attached to the Life line often suggests a susceptibility to gynaecological problems (ranging from irregular menstrual cycles to the need for a hysterectomy), and uro-genital problems (say, a tendency to hernia – congenital or acquired – or diseases affecting the testes or the urological system) in men. Emphasis must be placed on susceptibility, as many with the marking have no such complications. If problems were to develop, other markings, such as stars or islands in appropriate places on the Life or Head lines, would also be present.

Markings in the lines

Any fault in a line spells an obstruction to that line's energies. The nature of the obstruction obviously depends on what that specific line represents. Timing the line on which the fault occurs will show the onset and duration of events symbolized by the marking.

Island

An island in a line denotes a lowering of energy levels. Throughout the duration of an island, vitality and resistance are low. By timing and measuring the line and the length of the island, it is possible to calculate when the lowered resistance is likely to occur and how long it might last. Depending on its position, an island can point to specific areas of concern and may either indicate a temporary state, lasting only for the duration of the island, or a general predisposition to a particular disease.

Chain

This series of islands indicates poor vitality. Within the major lines, chains may be a sign of mineral deficiencies.

Break

Any breaks in a line show change. The strength and direction of the section of line after the break will reveal the nature of that change.

Although a break is usually interpreted as a change in personal or psychological circumstances, certain breaks in the Heart or Life lines can suggest serious health problems.

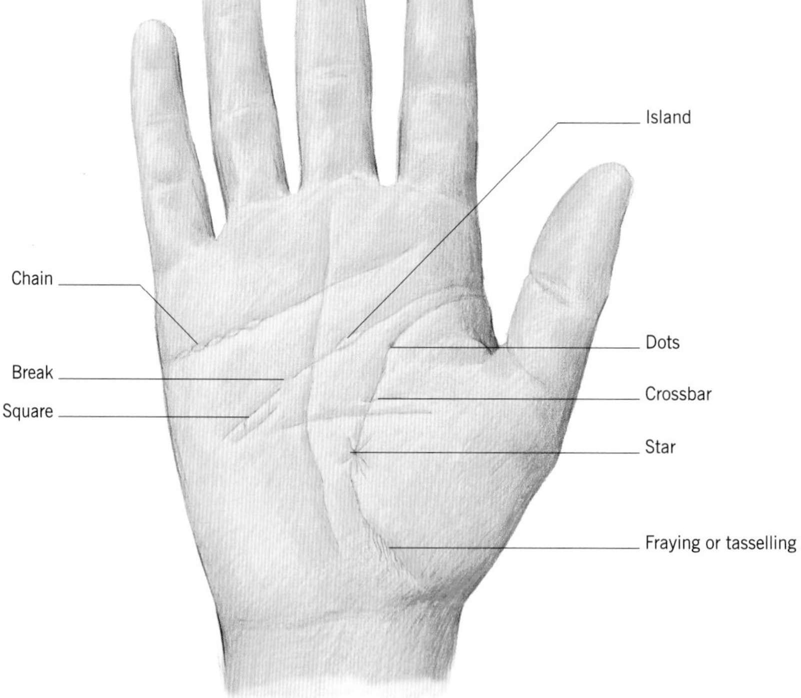

Island

Chain

Break

Square

Dots

Crossbar

Star

Fraying or tasselling

Crossbar

These usually act like a dam in a river, stopping the energy flow. The longer, stronger and thicker the crossbar, the greater the obstruction. This marking usually indicates a temporary set-back and examining the condition of the line after the crossbar determines whether the obstruction has left long-term damage. If, immediately after the bar, the main line picks up with the same strength as before, then recovery should be fairly swift; if it shows further weaknesses, the set-back may have greater consequences.

Star

A tiny 'star-burst' cluster – small crossbars crossing a line in the same place – suggests a shock to the system. However, stars that are found on the mounts, independent of any lines, are usually positive markings that are concerned with character and disposition rather than health.

Square

Four little lines in a square, directly over the line or adjoining it by one of its sides, is often

Health notes

Flaring – fine lines rising from the centre of the palm towards the ring and little fingers – denotes a susceptibility to gastric and intestinal problems. A poor diet or anxiety are common underlying causes.

a sign of protection. A square over a break, for example, may mitigate against the break's adverse effects. However, a square may point to stressful increased workloads for the duration of the marking, or its boxy shape may symbolize constriction of some kind.

Dots

Spots, dots or tiny indentations show a period of mental stress. How this will affect your general health depends on where the actual markings appear.

Fraying or tasselling

This 'feathering' towards the end of a main line denotes a frittering away of vitality. Be warned not to overdo things – consolidate your strengths until your energy levels return.

Compare and contrast

When analysing markings on major lines, always study all other markings and lines in the hands, especially to compare the other major lines at the same point in time. Secondly, check the appearance of the line immediately following the marking. If strong and clear, lasting detrimental effect is unlikely. If, however, the other main lines show similar indications, and the line you are studying is impaired after the marking, preventative action, such as improving diet and attitude, should be taken – you may even find the negative markings disappearing!

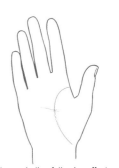

Change in line following effects represented by a marking

The Head line

Our minds have a powerful effect over our health. A positive attitude helps our bodies to heal themselves; the mind can also trigger the release of chemicals that cause bodily reactions. These vital mental processes are registered in minute detail in our Head lines, which also provide information on our mental health and the condition of the head and brain, including inherited genetic conditions.

Psychological indications

The ideal beginning for a Head line is one that just touches the Life line or at least lies very slightly apart. This shows a well-balanced disposition. One that begins inside the Life line tends to denote a clingy and dependent person who is timid, sensitive, anxious and withdrawn. These traits also apply to the Head line that is joined to the Life line for a long way, not breaking free until almost beneath the middle finger. These are life's late developers. Beginning widely separated from the Life line suggests a high degree of independence, sense of adventure, even foolhardy recklessness (putting these people at greater risk from accidents), especially when young.

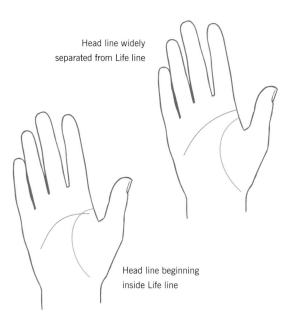

Head line widely separated from Life line

Head line beginning inside Life line

————	Head
- - - -	Life

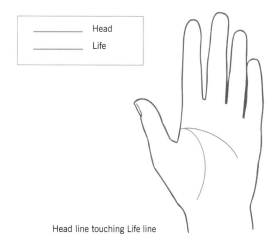

Head line touching Life line

Physiological indication

The Head line also registers the actual physical condition of the head, skull, brains, neck and upper torso. Physical injuries and diseases that affect these areas (fevers, headaches, dementia, paralysis or strokes, for example) will be marked on this line and discussed in the relevant section.

Length

The length of the Head line does not reflect your intelligence. The line's texture – in relation to the hand type in question – and its direction across your palm are the factors more relevant to IQ.

What your Head line says about you

Clear and well-etched
This is the ideal Head line, which should also be neither too deep nor too shallow and preferably without any defects or detrimental markings. Such a line reflects an even-tempered individual who is able to take the demands of modern life in their stride.

A wide, shallow line
These people are not very good at channelling their energies constructively. Indecision and a lack of concentration are characteristic.

A thin, wispy line
Like a thin wire, people with this line are easily snapped. Avoid taking on too much pressure because you will easily buckle – nervous exhaustion is always a threat here.

As with the other main lines, the texture of the Head line should be compatible with the type of hand in which it occurs because, a conflict would set up tensions that could lead to stress-related diseases. So a strong, fairly straight line would be expected on an Earth hand; a clear, distinct line with a springy curve is associated with both the Air and Fire categories; while a much finer, more curved Head line suits the Water hand.

Straight and curved lines

A line that travels horizontally straight across the palm denotes a positive, logical, analytical, sometimes dyed-in-the-wool mentality. Straight and short lines are associated with practical, materialistic, somewhat single-minded people – perhaps rather narrow in outlook and resistant to change, or even obsessional. The longer the line, the more mentally flexible the individual (and also the more open, in many cases, to complementary ways of treating their health).

A gently curved line reflects a creative, versatile mentality, someone who is open to new experiences and ideas. But if the line is too steeply curved, the imagination may be running wild, constructing an unrealistic fantasy world. Unless otherwise balanced out, mood disorders and mental illness are characteristic in these cases.

Hypersensitivity that verges on touchiness, pessimism, disappointment, neurosis and depression is associated with the long, steep Head line. So too are tendencies towards addiction and dependency, for this line shows a mentality open to suggestion.

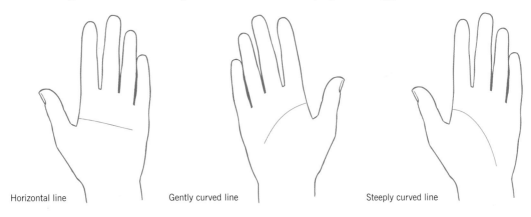

Horizontal line   Gently curved line   Steeply curved line

Markings in the Head line

Islands

These denote either a vulnerability to psychological problems or a set period of anxiety. An island in a line splits the flow of energy, so throughout the duration of an island in the Head line the owner's mental powers are not firing on all four cylinders. Decisions become difficult to make, with woolly-mindedness and a lack of concentration.

An island can be timed and so will pinpoint fairly accurately when your mental energy is likely to run at a low ebb, helping you to avoid the worst. A comparison with the other major lines will highlight the nature of the problem – if adverse markings are corroborated on your Fate line, for example, perhaps it is related to dissatisfaction at work.

Islands may be present in cases where the Head line begins attached to the Life line. As with the Life line, these can denote either susceptibility to bronchial and respiratory disorders or show psychological problems in childhood.

It is common to find an island halfway along the Head line, directly beneath the middle finger, signalling that its owner finds it difficult to work under pressure. They must learn to pace themselves in stressful scenarios, or their health will suffer. If an island is present towards the end of the Head line, it may represent the sort of mental conditions that often accompany old age – from forgetfulness and anxiety to senile dementia.

A chain of islands in the Head line warns against overtaxing one's mental reserves because these are at a low ebb for the duration of a chain, making the owner more vulnerable to health troubles. It is possible that a mineral imbalance could be an underlying factor – in which case diet might be investigated, as the sodium/potassium balance in the body could be out of kilter.

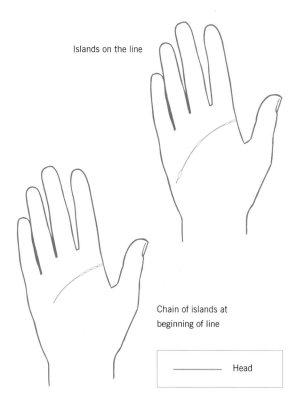

Islands on the line

Chain of islands at beginning of line

——— Head

Health notes

When an island is present in the Head line of the passive hand but not in that of the dominant one, the source of the anxiety is likely to be an emotional problem. A certain subtle malaise is characteristic – not causing any great disruption or trauma, but grumbling away in the background. The major danger here is in bottling up one's feelings, with all the psychological disorders that such repression can bring.

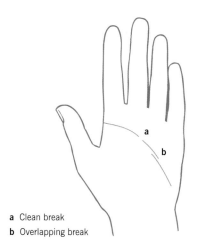

a Clean break
b Overlapping break

Health notes

Protection markings that
may appear over a defect
on the line include a
square (bringing hope of a
good recovery) and a sister
line – a small section of
line that lies beside the
fault (representing a shoring
up of the energies).

Breaks

A clean break in the line, with no overlapping
ends, may represent a physical injury to the head
itself. Confirmation of this would be marked in
the Life line at the corresponding time and the
construction of the line directly after the mark
will reveal how the individual will respond to
the situation. When the ends overlap, the
marking is less likely to refer to a physical event;
a major change in attitude is more likely.

Cross

A cross on the line has the same meaning as the
star, but only when clearly marked and deeply

Fuzzy line

A broad line with a fluffy or fuzzy appearance
denotes woolly-mindedness and inability to make
clear-cut decisions. Perhaps there is simply too
much going on in the individual's life throughout
the period marked on the line in this way.

Quite often, such fuzziness appears in just one
short section of line. It's common to see this, for
example, in the part of the line that represents a
woman's child-bearing years. Here, the fuzziness
equates with the draining effect of a hectic family
life. Or it might be seen later on in her hand –
during the menopause, say – when the body is
in a state of flux. During the time when the Head
line is formed into this fluffiness, forgetfulness
and tiredness are hazards to health, energies are
depleted and the constitution bears the brunt,
with increased vulnerability to disease.

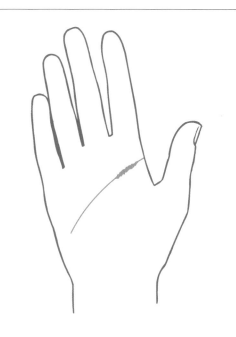

engraved. The cross, however, must be made up of independent, free-standing lines and not by main lines, such as the Fate, for instance, whose normal course takes it over the Head line.

Crossbars

Bars cutting the Head line suggest obstacles and set-backs. These are likely to affect psychological well-being rather than physical health.

Star

A star formation implies a shock to the system. On the Head line, it can suggest a susceptibility to stroke. Whichever applies will be confirmed by markings elsewhere. As always, the section of line directly after the star highlights how the owner is likely to be mentally and physically affected.

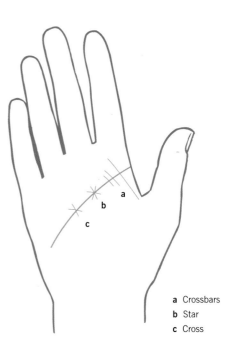

a Crossbars
b Star
c Cross

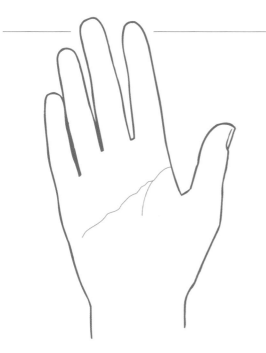

Dips and zigzags

A dip in the Head line suggests a time of depression. This is all the more likely if a small line sweeps out from the lowest point of the dip and shoots downwards. The likely onset and duration of the depression can be measured and timed with a timing gauge, giving enough notice for the situation to be dealt with before any ill-effects are felt.

In some hands, the Head line forms a noticeable zigzag as it travels across the palm. This represents a vascillating mentality, with constructive periods when the line rises and a lull when it falls. These switchback periods can be accurately measured and timed by applying the timing gauge. If, on the descent, the line also forms itself into little dips, it suggests that its owner has a tendency to slide into spells of depression.

Head

The Simian and Sydney lines

These two lines are exceptional forms of the Head line and have a specific bearing on mental health.

The Simian line

This forms when the Heart and Head lines fuse to form one solid crease that cuts horizontally across the centre of the hand. Found in only a few people, it is commonly associated with Down's syndrome and other conditions caused by abnormal chromosomes that may lead to physical and mental impairment. In these cases it may be accompanied by very short, pointed fingers, small thumbs or displaced skin-ridge patterns.

In a normal hand, the line denotes an ambitious, restless and intense personality – an individual who views everything in black and white and finds it difficult to switch off. With extremely high standards, they drive themselves – and others – hard and are demanding and jealous if they feel their partners are disloyal or not demonstrative enough. Such people often experience a conflict between their emotions and their intellectual drives, leading many to some degree of compulsive behaviour.

Physiological indications
Heart defects may be suspected when a Simian line is accompanied by a complete set of fingertip arches and a displaced axial triradius pattern (see page 57). In fact, just a triradius occurring higher up on the palm in the area governed by the Head line is sufficient to alert one's attention to cardiac problems, whether a Simian line is present in the hand or not.

The Sydney line

The Sydney line is a Head line that stretches across the palm from one edge to the other, but is independent of the Heart line. In the abnormal hand, it can show a tendency towards behavioural problems such as aggressive tendencies, emotional disorders, learning difficulties and hyperactivity.

Dots and indentations

Pin-prick indentations signal susceptibility to headaches, especially migraines, or sinus problems, or may simply warn you that such conditions run in your family. These dots often appear in clusters, denoting a particularly bad time for such attacks. A single dot tells of an acute attack, such as a dangerously high fever, that temporarily affects the brain.

Fraying

A tassel effect towards the end of the Head line suggests mental impairment caused by a draining of cerebral function. Forgetfulness, senile dementia and Alzheimer's disease might all be represented in this way.

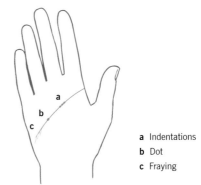

a Indentations
b Dot
c Fraying

The Heart line

This line tells the story of our emotions – and also helps to reveal how healthy our cardiovascular system is. Markings here can point to genetic, or 'wired-in', conditions as well as give clues to potential developments – both negative and positive – which will have a direct effect on the heart and circulation of its owner.

Psychological indications

The important factors here are whether the line is curved or straight, plus its length and ending point.

A straight Heart line denotes someone who is cool and undemonstrative, but very much in control of their emotions, while a curved line shows a warm, demonstrative person who is not afraid to wear their heart on their sleeve.

In romantic matters, owners of straight lines are emotionally passive, while those with curved lines are said to be sexy and active. Straight-liners will probably be very rational in their choice of partner, carefully weighing up the pros and cons before committing themselves. Within the relationship, they will most likely want a strong mental understanding and this will be more important to them than the sexual aspect. If you possess a curved line, emotional and sexual love will be essential – you must be physically turned on by your partner before committing yourself.

Lying higher or lower in the palm will also reveal the individual's instinctive response in relationships. The nearer to the fingers the line is situated, the more self-centred the nature; the lower down the palm, the warmer, more generous and caring the individual is towards others.

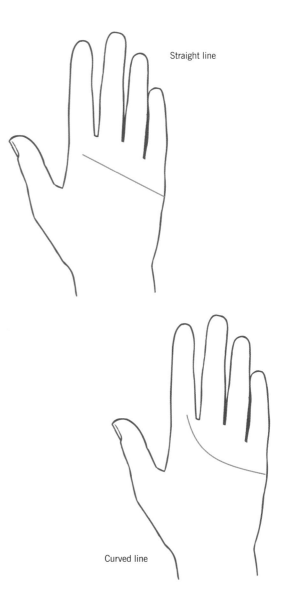

Straight line

Curved line

Common line endings

Unless modified by other markings in the hand, there is no true warmth of feeling or love here (except for oneself, that is), nor a desire to share with anyone else.

A line ending beneath the middle finger is considered short and is found on those who crave personal sexual gratification – sex is more important than love, one-night stands preferred to longer-lasting relationships. These people almost have an abhorrence of being 'tied down' with someone.

If you have this type of line, you will find it difficult to express your innermost feelings verbally to the people you love. For you, doing is more important than saying.

A line that ends high on the webbing between the first and second fingers must naturally be curved and so belongs to the active-lover category. With this line, however, although the disposition is loving, giving and demonstrative, affection is shown through actions rather than by the voicing of feelings.

If you own one of these you are a perfectionist, driving yourself hard and expecting others to do so as well.

If the line reaches up and touches the base of the index finger, expect extremely high standards of excellence and even higher expectations in all relationships. Unless modified elsewhere in your hand, possessive jealousy is one of your downfalls.

Owners of this type of line are often let down in relationships and love simply because their ideals are unattainable.

Ending beneath the index finger, right in the middle of the mount of Jupiter, this highlights the eternal romantic who sees everything through rose-tinted spectacles. There is an idealistic approach to love, and relationships and unrealistic expectations.

Many of these people will be found on various committees, shouldering responsibilities, helping in the community.

People whose Heart lines travel across the palm, underneath the index mount to almost touch the other edge, tend to want to care for others. Some may put their work before their own emotional needs.

A well-balanced sign where romance is concerned.

Branched endings, where the line splits into two or even three, shows a well-balanced attitude to emotions and relationships.

Owners of this line get easily hurt when love affairs go wrong.

A Heart line that turns down at its end and falls onto the Head line is the sign of a very sensitive nature, where relationships are concerned.

Physiological indications

Unusual formations and major deformities in the Heart line are associated with genetic and congenital problems and are often found in people born with severe physical handicaps. Actual defects within the cardiac system or a susceptibility to heart disease may also be represented in this way, or by negative markings in the line beneath the ring and little fingers. However, as mentioned earlier, such formations would also be accompanied by other corroborative markings.

Length

The length of the line in no way relates to longevity, and timing age and events on this line has been found unreliable. Markings such as islands and crossbars in the line cannot be correlated in time but may be translated against the other major lines. In fact, quite often a bar or a fine line will connect a marking on the Heart line to one of the other main lines, making it possible to assess the likely onset of the problem by timing the second line.

Detecting heart disease

The sort of markings that would accompany a susceptibility to cardiovascular problems or to heart disease are well documented, but vary from hand to hand and from person to person. In general, however, one might expect to find a bluish discoloration to the skin, particularly at the base of the nails. Bulbous fingertips, possibly with severely humped nails, might also be present. Fan-shaped nails are a common sign of a tendency to circulatory problems, as are unusual fingerprints or displaced skin-ridge patterns such as a highly placed axial triradius (see page 57). Of course, severely malformed Heart lines would lead one to suspect damage due to genetic or congenital defects.

Markings in the Heart line

Islands

These occur naturally in most Heart lines as they enter the palm at the percussion edge. But if a single large island is found on the line beneath the little or ring finger, especially if it is noticeably blue or reddish, it may denote a susceptibility to heart disease. A single island that lies in the section of line situated beneath the middle finger has been associated with hearing problems.

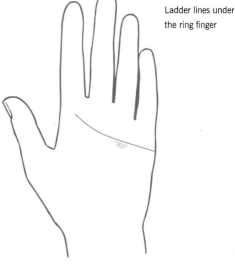

Ladder lines under the ring finger

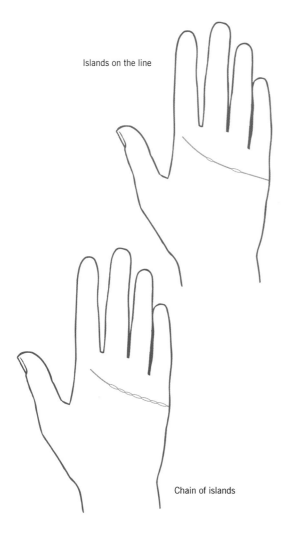

Islands on the line

Chain of islands

Psychologically, islanding or chaining (groups of islands) in the Heart line suggests nervous or emotional tension. Physiologically, chaining that runs along most of the length is associated with cardiac and circulatory conditions such as irregularities in heartbeat rhythm (bringing symptoms such as palpitations). Similar to the Head line, the chaining formation here may also suggest an imbalance of sodium and potassium.

Ladder lines

Sometimes, a ladder-like series of tiny lines, dropping from the Heart line directly beneath the ring finger, is associated with a deficiency of calcium fluoride or with an imbalance of calcium/magnesium levels. Insomnia, altered or disturbed sleep patterns, anxiety and nervousness may all be symptomatic of this type of deficiency.

Breaks

A break in the Heart line needs careful analysis, for here the marking can be very serious. If the line looks as if it has been snapped in two beneath the ring finger – and if there are corroborating features such as irregular skin-ridge markings, and blueness of the nails and/or fingertips – there could be implicit cardiovascular problems, tendencies to coronary disease or even danger of a heart attack. If you ever suspect that you have detected this feature you would be very wise (without giving cause for alarm) to suggest that its owner get a full medical check-up from their doctor.

Bars

Any bars that cut across the line show temporary impediments and also emotional set-backs.

Health notes

Veiling on the percussion is when the area around the edge of the palm beneath the Heart line appears heavily crisscrossed by fine lines. It implies a predisposition to rheumatic complaints. Some believe the veiling is caused by a build-up of uric acid, which is sometimes implicated in gouty or rheumatic illnesses.

Star

A star is never a good sign, and on this line it may indicate either a huge emotional upset or the possibility of a heart attack. Markings on the other major lines would, of course, have to corroborate these findings.

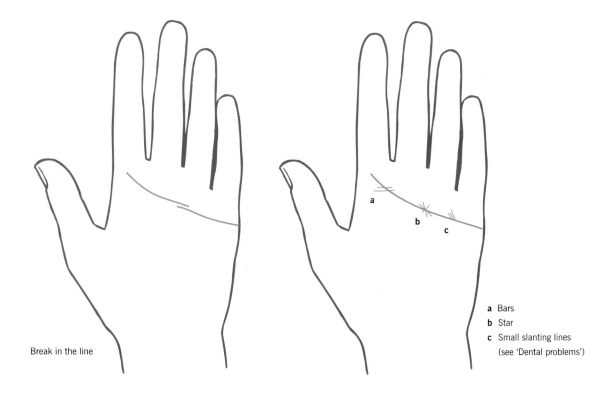

Break in the line

a Bars
b Star
c Small slanting lines
(see 'Dental problems')

Dental problems

Gum disease, tooth decay and general orthodontal problems are sometimes represented by a group of tiny slanting lines that lie just above the Heart line beneath the little finger. The same set of lines can equally reflect problems with the stomach, intestines and liver. This situation may arise because gum disease is in some cases caused by stomach or liver dysfunction, or because the latter can cause poor dentition – this is very much a chicken-and-egg situation. Care must be taken not to confuse these lines with the Medical Stigmata (see pages 35 and 100).

Health notes

Little hard lumps can sometimes develop on or around the Heart line beneath the ring finger either prior to a heart attack or immediately following one. These nodules are quite noticeable, as they tend to distort the course of the Heart line and feel like bumpy scar tissue. They should not be confused with calluses, often present in this area of the palm, nor with the tendons and knucklebones that lie deep within the palm at the root of the ring finger.

Branches in the line

A branch that sweeps out of the Heart line and drops onto the Head line may be interpreted as a sign of a sensitive nature. (The Heart line that itself wilts onto the Head line at its ending gives the same sign.) However, if the branch sweeps out and hits, not the beginning of the Head line, but some point along its course, it could well be alluding to a major emotional upset. This event can be timed on the Head line, where other confirmatory markings will probably be found.

Two parallel branches that shoot out of the Heart line beneath the little and ring fingers and then sweep down towards the Luna mount are said to denote a predisposition to strokes and paralysis.

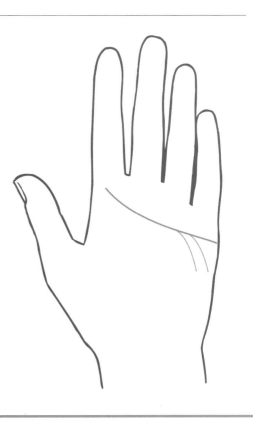

A question of timing

The ability to time potential future events accurately has obvious health benefits, enabling hand analysts to counsel people to take preventive steps. However, timing dates and events on the lines can be tricky because hands come in all shapes and sizes. It isn't possible to apply the same scale to all people, so it must be customized for each individual hand – difficult until you have had some experience. Fortunately, there is a fail-safe system that all the experts recommend. Look for a clear marking registering a significant

Timing on the different lines

Use the Life, Head and Fate lines for timing – the Heart and secondary lines are not reliable.

Timing events on the Life line
Draw a vertical line downwards from the inside edge of the index finger to the Life line. This point is roughly 20 years of age. One year of life is represented on the line by about one millimetre (perhaps a generous millimetre for a large hand, slightly less than a millimetre for a small one). Working from the 20-year mark, each rough millimetre towards the edge of the palm takes us back in time, and each one towards the wrist adds on one more year.

Timing events on the Head line
The vertical line is again dropped from the inside edge of the index finger to strike the

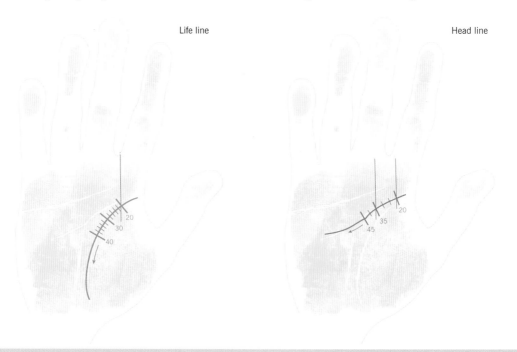

Life line

Head line

event in the subject's past, time it using a timing gauge (see instructions below) and then simply ask the individual to confirm it. If you're a year or two out, adjust the scale to fit, and check it by reapplying it to another major mark.

Though it is possible to measure the lines and make quick mental calculations when the actual hand is spread out in front of you, it is perhaps more advisable to take a clear print and work from that (see 'Taking handprints', pages 10–11).

Head line at 20. The same rule of 'one millimetre to a year' is applied, working backwards towards the thumb edge through adolescence and childhood, and forwards across the palm from 20 onwards. An additional check can be made by dropping a vertical line from the centre of the middle finger onto the Head line – this point should touch at around 35 years.

Timing events on the Fate line

The Fate line is treated differently, principally because it has such a variety of starting points. Because of this, the best method is to measure the palm itself, which is at least a constant, and then transfer that measurement across to the line.

Measure the palm by drawing a vertical line from the top 'bracelet' at the wrist to the base of the middle finger. Mark a point halfway up this vertical line – this is the 35-year point. Again, use the millimetre-a-year rule to divide it up. A little poetic licence has to be used because each millimetre is a generous one between 0 and 35, but compressed from 35 onwards so that each year is represented by slightly less than a millimetre. Draw horizontal lines across from the vertical line to transfer the points to the Fate line.

Fate line

55
45
35
25
15

_____ Life	_____ Fate
_____ Head	

The Fate line

From an analytical point of view, the Fate line tracks and records our way of life – our movements and major life changes, attitudes to work, sociability, influences that alter our lives, our need for security and, because it is also known as the line of Saturn, how we actually deal with responsibility.

Psychological indications

The Fate line represents how much control we feel we have over what happens to us, our immediate environment and our destinies. Personal control is essential to psychological well-being. Without it we lose motivation, we retreat anxiously inside ourselves and basically give up.

The Fate line registers the degree of control we feel we can exert. And it is from the point in our palms that the line first appears that we feel we start to pick up the reins firmly. The stronger the line appears, the more control we feel we have. However, the actual quality of the line must match the type of hand in which it is found, otherwise some personality conflicts may arise.

Physiological indications

Though not directly considered to reflect physical problems, a strong Fate line behaves as an insurance policy to the Life line, shoring up its weaknesses.

Another way to look at the Fate line is to see it as a column or ridge pole supporting a structure, such as a canopy, let's say. Like the column, a strong, well-etched Fate line shows that its owner is capable of taking the load – or, in other words, carrying responsibility. The weaker the line, the less responsible the individual is likely to be.

Health notes

For the few who don't possess a Fate line at all, this doesn't necessarily mean a dull, uninteresting life. They can be just as successful as the next person – as long as the other main lines are strong and well-formed. But lacking this line can mean that its owner takes a non-conventional, unpredictable approach to life, not caring too much for rules, commitment or security, and can denote irresponsibility, even untrustworthiness. Those who lack the line and whose hands show other negative features may choose to live a life outside the law. From the little research that has been carried out in this area, there is some evidence to suggest that a good percentage of delinquents, misfits and people with psychopathic tendencies lack a Fate line.

Length

Ideally, this line should stretch from the base of the palm right up to the base of the fingers, with no breaks or defects. In fact, Fate lines of all lengths are found, and are sometimes missing altogether. Though this line can be measured and timed accurately, its length in no way equates with the owner's longevity.

Strong and weak lines

These people have plenty of drive and ambition, feel they can exert influence and make their own opportunities, and are generally in control of their lives.

A strong Fate line

This is usually found in the hands of people with a good self-concept – those with a healthy amount of self-esteem who understand their worth and standing in life. Indomitable, with masses of willpower, they possess the capacity to achieve whatever goal they set their sights on and can sustain any weaknesses that might appear in the other main lines. This type of line represents an excellent support system for any mental, emotional or physical problems that might arise.

With low self-esteem, these people tend to be more emotionally immature, dependent and submissive, more inclined to let things happen rather than take the initiative.

A line that is very broken and twisted is also a weak line.

A faint or weak Fate line

This reveals someone who lacks inner strength, is not particularly resourceful, and who doesn't possess a strong self-image. And, because their supporting 'ridge pole' is in danger of collapsing if any undue pressure is put upon them, they are more vulnerable to psychiatric disorders, psychosomatic problems and physical disease, especially if the other main lines are also weak or negatively marked.

A fragmented Fate line

There is a great deal of indecision, of stopping and starting, implied here. In some hands, the Fate line begins in this fragmented fashion because it reveals a time when an individual is trying to find their feet in life. If the line strengthens up further along, it suggests that they do indeed find a purpose.

If an otherwise strong line breaks up into fragments somewhere along its course, it is likely that some event has thrown the individual badly off the rails. The other lines should be checked for confirmatory negative markings such as depression and traumatic upsets. If the line eventually mends itself, the owner regains their equilibrium. Beginnings, duration and endings of such occurrences can be timed (see 'Timing events on the Fate line', page 89).

Start and finish

It is the beginning and ending points of the Fate line that shed significant information.

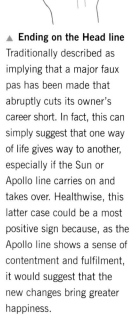

▲ **Starting attached to the Life line**
A classic indication of early family responsibilities. Just as the line itself is tethered to the Life line, so these people are tied to their families from an early age, perhaps caring for a sick parent or having to leave school early to work to support their families. There is a sense of restriction and dependency that may last well into adult life.

▲ **Starting further up in the palm**
This suggests that a true sense of purpose and stability, and success, are not achieved until later on in life.

▲ **Starting from the centre of the palm at the wrist and shooting straight up to Saturn**
This denotes a solid, responsible individual with traditional values and a somewhat fatalistic turn of mind. These people like to preplan everything they do in life, and perhaps prefer a 'safe' life with few risks.

▲ **Starting at the mount of Luna**
This denotes a sociable, caring outlook – someone who is happiest around other people, who doesn't like being on their own, and enjoys life in the limelight.

▲ **Ending beneath the middle finger**
This is the most common ending. The Fate line is otherwise known as the line of Saturn, and this is its most fitting destination, because the middle digit is called the finger of Saturn and the area beneath, upon which the line normally comes to rest, is the Saturn mount.

▲ **Ending on the Jupiter mount**
A life and career led among people is suggested here, especially caring for others in the community or dealing with the general public and achieving some standing – a doctor or local councillor, for instance.

▲ **Swinging over to end on the Apollo mount**
This shows a turning towards a more creatively fulfilling way of life, and thus one that promotes contentment and peace of mind.

▲ **Ending on the Head line**
Traditionally described as implying that a major faux pas has been made that abruptly cuts its owner's career short. In fact, this can simply suggest that one way of life gives way to another, especially if the Sun or Apollo line carries on and takes over. Healthwise, this latter case could be a most positive sign because, as the Apollo line shows a sense of contentment and fulfilment, it would suggest that the new changes bring greater happiness.

▲ **Ending on the Heart line**
Here, the traditional explanation is also that a major emotional blunder has terminated the career. But if similar markings to the above are present, what might at first appear as a negative outcome might turn out to be a general improvement to its owner's well-being.

Markings in the Fate line

Because this line represents our way of life in all its aspects, any markings are extremely important. Also, the Fate line acts as a support to the other main lines, the Life line in particular, so its markings will shed light on information gleaned from the other major lines. And, finally, this line can be timed with a very good degree of accuracy, which means that it can provide a pretty good idea of the onset and duration of events, states of mind or whatever that may influence our daily lives.

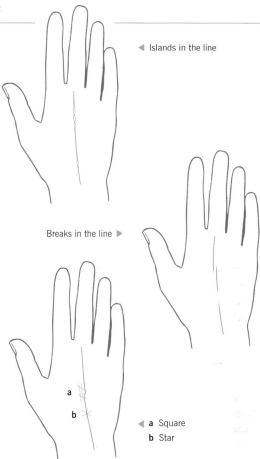

◄ Islands in the line

Breaks in the line ►

a
b

◄ a Square
  b Star

Islands

This usually denotes a period of dissatisfaction and frustration with work or life in general, or perhaps a period of financial difficulties or other restrictions. Whatever problem is being highlighted should also be marked on the other main lines, and in some cases is linked to them by a fine line – as if directing attention to the source. A chained formation turns the line into a weak one, and also lessens its ability to support any of the other lines.

Breaks

Any breaks in this line show a change either in work or domestic circumstances. If it is a clean break, the change has been enforced. If the two ends overlap, the change is made at the owner's instigation. For example, redundancy may be represented by the former, while applying for and getting a new job might describe the latter. Studying the condition of the line following the break and comparing the other lines for the same period is essential in establishing what effects these changes may have.

A break in the Fate line may not have the same impact on all types of people. People with Earth and Fire hands might find the effects of a break more disruptive than Air or Water types, who are more tolerant of change and variety.

Star

This warning sign can denote a time of crisis – a nervous breakdown, a sudden attack or an unexpected piece of bad news, perhaps.

Square

This alerts its owner to a period of hard work, when greater responsibilities must be shouldered. Positively, this industrious phase is a time of consolidation, when future foundations are laid.

Line colour

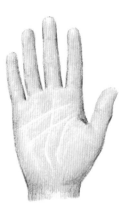

▲ When either major or minor lines are very red (and not due to race or increased activity), it is a sign of a fiery temperament and feverish conditions or cardiovascular problems.

▲ Yellowy lines in a European hand may suggest liver problems, and jaundice in particular.

▲ Lines that appear pale, or run white when the fingers are flexed back and the skin across the palm stretched, may signify a deficiency of iron. Many women find that their lines tend to lose colour during, and a few days following, menstruation, as a direct result of iron loss. Increased intake of iron alone may not always be sufficient to redress the balance. When the white lines persist, it could be that magnesium and Vitamin B6 are deficient. Vitamins belonging to the B-complex group, and Vitamins C and E, may help in many cases, while folic acid can aid the absorption and assimilation of iron.

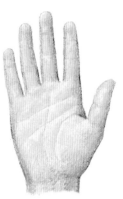

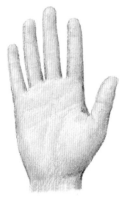

▲ Generally speaking, pale lines show that vitality and physical resources are low. Rest and an improved diet containing a good balance of vitamins and minerals should be enough to restore the lines to their normal colour.

▲ Sometimes, in certain terminal diseases, the lines may fade away. This has also been found to occur in cases of severe copper deficiency. However, this condition is unlikely to be found among the world's wealthier nations.

Lines have also been found to disappear in rare cases where physical damage has occurred to the brain, reappearing once health is restored. Yet, remarkably, the hands of mummified bodies, dead for thousands of years, have been found still bearing signs of their major lines.

Indications in the Minor Lines

The Health line

A well-defined Health line implies that, like a finely tuned barometer, you are able to pick up and monitor, with fine precision, the state of your own health at any given moment in time. We've discussed the fact that lines can and do change – well, this line is more subject to change than any other. In times of stress, for example, the line may become longer or deeper. Within a matter of days, the proper treatment, enough rest, and even the smallest improvement to one's way of life, can make an enormous difference to the line's condition.

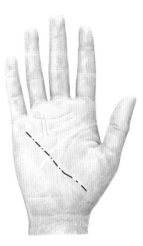

Psychological indications

The Health line is most valuable as an indicator of physiological disorders although, having said that, it will inevitably reflect the particular state of mind that accompanies our physical health at any given time. For example, because acidity, ulcers, indigestion and other general gastric conditions may be caused by nervous tension, the Health line can be consulted for corroboration of nervous fatigue or stress-related problems that have first been picked up on the other main lines.

Physiological indications

Most hand analysts agree that the best Health line to possess is, in fact, no Health line at all. As our Health line shows our awareness of our personal health, then you could argue that not possessing it is perhaps better for us than having it. If we do have a Health line, it is best to have a strong, long and unblemished one, as this reflects a robust, vital constitution and good resistance to illness. A clear line that shows very few defects also suggests that both the metabolism and immune system are in impressive working order.

Length

Line length varies from hand to hand and does not equate with longevity. Any illnesses marked in this line will be found to have corresponding signs on other major lines – the Life line in particular – and may be timed there (see page 88).

Health notes

A very red line may suggest that toxins are present and that the system is working hard at fighting them off. (See also 'Line colour', opposite.)

Markings in the line

Although defects, markings, twisting or fragmentation of the Health line give us a fair idea that our systems are under stress, they are not necessarily specific to particular organs or diseases. However, most defects will be found to suggest a dysfunction in the organs of digestion and elimination, including intestinal and gastric disorders, kidney and liver dysfunction, and respiratory and gynaecological ailments. For greater accuracy, markings are usually found to have their counterpart somewhere else in the hand, particularly in the major lines.

Remember – never take any single marking in isolation. Hand analysis works on multiple levels: each clue will be clarified and confirmed at every stage, and must be corroborated by a series of other features.

Islands

These show a period when the constitution is running at a low ebb, or indicate the duration of an illness. They also suggest a predisposition to chest infections and problems with the respiratory system. A chained line indicates general debility and a weakened constitution, and may suggest that the immune system is under stress.

Breaks

A broken or highly fragmented Health line is often a sign of general ill-health – the specific aspect under stress will be marked elsewhere. The broken Health line can also indicate stomach and liver problems, especially when a much-fragmented line forms a little ladder rising up the palm.

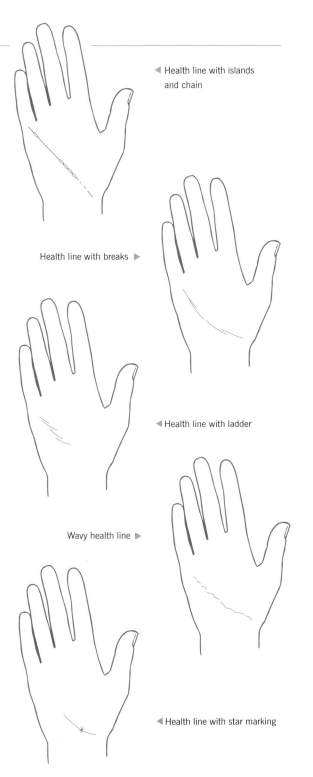

◀ Health line with islands and chain

Health line with breaks ▶

◀ Health line with ladder

Wavy health line ▶

◀ Health line with star marking

Twists and waves

A twisted or wavy Health line is normally associated with stomach, liver, gall bladder or intestinal problems. Digestive complaints are especially likely to be evident if the Health line begins on the mount of Venus, inside the Life line.

Star

This suggests a possible shock, acute illness, or perhaps the need for an urgent operation. If a star formation occurs at the point where the Health line crosses the Head line, this may denote the possibility of stroke or a gynaecological problem.

Venus, Allergy and fingertip lines

Girdle of Venus

People possessing this marking are generally highly creative, imaginative types. However, they may turn that imagination inwards to produce dark, brooding, unhealthy obsessions and hypochondria, making them prone to psychosomatic ailments.

Psychological indications

The line denotes a highly anxious, nervous individual who may become neurotic.

Physiological indications

The line is associated with psychological disorders rather than with physical illnesses.

Length

The line is best if in fragmented form and better still if non-existent. It is in no way associated with longevity.

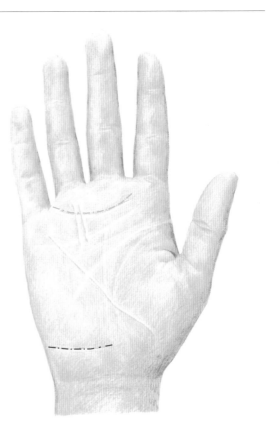

—·—·—	Allergy
— — — —	Girdle of Venus

The Allergy line

Psychological indications
Common in hyperactive children and addicts.

Physiological indications
When present, this line denotes a delicate physiological system that is especially sensitive to potential allergens such as drugs, airborne pollutants and alcohol. The line simply suggests that a sensitivity exists it does not highlight the specific allergen. In order to find that out, the owners could perhaps keep records of their diet and note any chemicals they come into contact with, together with their reactions. In serious cases, a desensitization programme or an elimination or detoxification diet might prove useful – as long as these are carefully monitored by medical practitioners or professional nutritionists or dietitians.

Line construction

- The ideal line, be it a major or minor one, should be clearly etched, neither too thick nor too thin, and free from any marking or defect.
- Thick, deeply chiselled lines show robust physical health. However, this type of line suggests a lack of control over one's strength and, though vitality is plentiful in short bursts, there is a tendency for it to burn itself out quickly. Such individuals must pace themselves and not throw all their reserves into whatever problem is immediately before them.
- Very thin, fine lines show a brittle vitality and suggest an inability to support great surges of energy when required. Owners of such lines may have poor physical or mental resources so that, if extra demands are made upon them, they may well crack under the strain.
- Fuzzy or woolly lines show lack of concentration – an inability to focus energies constructively and a tendency to scatter abilities.

Fingertip lines

Horizontal lines on fingertips
Sometimes called white lines, horizontal dashes across the fingertips are one of the first signs of stress and worry. These are some of the fastest lines to appear and disappear again as tension builds up and is released. Sometimes they can come and go within a matter of days, while at other times they remain on the fingertips – a witness to the fact that the problems are unresolved – for several years.

In some cases, a few random lines appear on the odd fingertip. In others, so many lines may develop that they almost obscure the ridge pattern on the finger – a warning that stress-related illness could develop if preventative steps are not taken in the near future. (See 'Fingertip markings', opposite.)

Vertical lines on fingertips
Evidence suggests that there is a relationship between the fingertips and the endocrine (hormonal) system. The tip of each finger, it is believed, reflects the condition of its specific corresponding endocrine gland.

Fingertip markings

Because each finger governs a particular facet of our lives, it is possible to determine the cause of stress by gauging which digits are most affected by these 'white' lines.

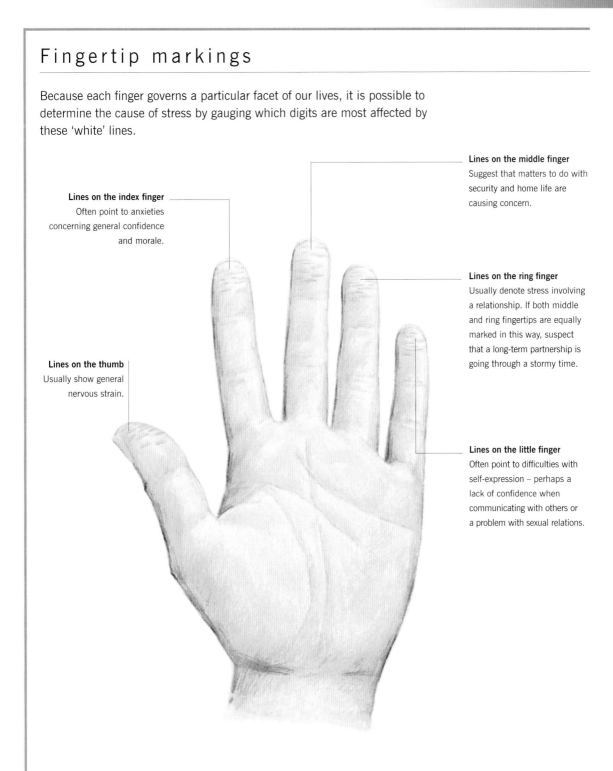

Lines on the middle finger
Suggest that matters to do with security and home life are causing concern.

Lines on the index finger
Often point to anxieties concerning general confidence and morale.

Lines on the ring finger
Usually denote stress involving a relationship. If both middle and ring fingertips are equally marked in this way, suspect that a long-term partnership is going through a stormy time.

Lines on the thumb
Usually show general nervous strain.

Lines on the little finger
Often point to difficulties with self-expression – perhaps a lack of confidence when communicating with others or a problem with sexual relations.

The body's endocrine glands release hormones into the bloodstream. Hormones either cause vital chemical changes themselves or trigger other glands into activity. Every part of a well-balanced glandular system secretes the correct amount of hormone according to the body's needs, and sends the correct messages to other glands to activate them. Should a gland malfunction, this chain reaction will go awry. It is this malfunctioning that is reflected by vertical lines running up from the top joint of the relevant finger.

Health notes

Tiredness lines are the strong vertical lines that run up the two basal phalanges of the fingers. When there are many of these lines present, it is a warning that the body is nearing exhaustion.

Other minor lines

The Medical Stigmata

When present, this three-line formation tells of a soothing and reassuring way of dealing with others, and a natural bent for the healing arts. Not all medical personnel possess the marking, but those who do have it stand out for their ability to empathize with patients. It may occur in anyone who is involved in any area of health, including counsellors and psychologists, and in all kinds of people who do not work in such fields at all.

Rascettes

These are the 'bracelet' markings or rings on the wrist. The average number of rings is about three, and the top one forms the boundary between the hand and the arm. On most arms, the bracelets form a neat horizontal line across the wrist, but in some cases the top ring arches up onto the palm – this is a sign of possible problems with childbirth.

Making the connections

Increasing evidence filters through to us from the ancient practices of shiatsu, acupuncture and reflexology to confirm a relationship between our internal organs and their corresponding external links. In hand analysis, however, evidence of these connections has started to be gathered only comparatively recently and a good deal more research needs to be done. So far, our understanding suggests the linkages highlighted below.

The tip of the ring finger

Said to be associated with the thymus, a gland that plays a major role in the immunological system. However, because the ring finger and the area on the palm directly below it are associated with the heart and circulation, it would seem more logical for vertical lines on this tip to reflect some malfunction of the cardiovascular system. Certainly, people with high blood pressure have also been found to possess heavily lined tips to their third fingers. As we knew little about the thymus until the 1960s, perhaps future researchers will establish a link between the thymus and the circulatory system. It is also worth noting that, in reflexology, the thymus link is found on the palm in a line directly beneath the ring finger.

The tip of the little finger

Connected to the thyroid gland, with much evidence to support this link. Vertical lines here can indicate over- or under-production of the hormone thyroxine, responsible for regulating metabolism. An imbalance of iodine, central to the production of the hormone, may be suspected in certain cases. Action of the thyroid gland is triggered by the pituitary.

The tip of the middle finger

Said to be linked to the pineal gland. We don't as yet know the exact function of this gland but suspect it plays a major role in maintaining our awareness of day and night and controlling our daily rhythms. Because this suggests that the pineal has a good deal to do with maintaining the body's balance, it would seem ideally placed on the Saturn fingertip, which corresponds to our sense of stabilization. Reflexology, however, sites this gland's terminal point in the thumb tip.

The tip of the index finger

Believed to correspond to the pituitary gland. This is the most important endocrine gland, as it produces essential hormones that control the activity of many other glands in the system. Interestingly, reflexology places the pituitary link in the thumb.

The tip of the thumb

This has not as yet had a glandular connection ascribed to it. In hand analysis, the top phalanx of this digit reflects our willpower and mental control over our lives. Isn't it interesting, then, that reflexology should recognize a connection between this area and the pituitary, the chief controller of the endocrine system? Reflexology also sites the pineal here and, as both pituitary and pineal glands are located in the brain, it would be logical for both glands to find their correspondence here, at the seat of mental control.

Your line type

It is essential to compare the lines that are found in a hand with whichever one of the four basic types that hand appears to be (see Part One, pages 16–17).

Earth

The practical Earth type is characterized by a few bold, firmly etched lines.
• If this hand contains very few, extremely strong and thick lines, the individual will be robust but could burn themselves out unless they channel their energy properly.
• Weak, broken lines here mean that the owner lacks the strength that their fundamental nature demands of them.
• A cobweb of fine lines here reflects a highly strung nature at variance with the basic Earth personality, giving rise to inner tension. It also denotes someone who cannot think imaginatively and also make those ideas reality (a typical Earth person is skilled at manual tasks).

Air

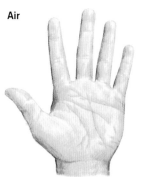

The lively and clever Air type tends to show a good few more lines than the Earth hand, but they are clear and well-formed, which gives the palm an uncluttered look.
• Too few lines suggests a lack of sensitivity, with creativity and intellectual appreciation suffering as a consequence.
• Too many lines, particularly if they are badly constructed, may suggest an element of neurosis.

Fire

The exuberant Fire type typically possesses many lines and, though the main ones will be strongly engraved, they may be interwoven by several minor ones that are often brittle and fragmented.
• The stronger the lines, the more the owner is able to focus their energies. Strong, well-cut lines here give good mental and physical resources, together with plenty of scope to bring plans to fruition.
• Too many fine lines, particularly if broken and poorly constructed, suggest a highly strung individual with too little control over the emotions – dangerous in one who lives in the fast lane. The individual judges badly and is impressionable.

Water

The hypersensitive Water type displays a profusion of lines, with the main ones finely formed and crisscrossed with numerous extraneous lines that are often thin and fragmented.
• The more lines here, the more highly strung the individual. Depression and mental instability is likely, even neurosis and obsessiveness. Though often highly creative, too many lines suggests poor concentration, so clever plans may never see the light of day.
• In the unlikely event of finding a Water hand with few lines, there will be greater determination to fulfil ambitions, although a certain cold-blooded ruthlessness may exist.

Full and empty hands

An instant clue to a person's well-being lies in the quantity of lines in the palm. A 'full' hand is crowded with a complex, confused cobweb of crisscrossing lines all over palm and fingers. The uncluttered 'empty' hand contains few, clear lines, often only the three or four major ones. Essentially, the more numerous and fine or brittle the lines, the more super-sensitive the individual, physically and psychologically.

Interestingly, although those with nervous energy seem physically more fragile, they can be rather tough and resilient, able to withstand difficult situations and painful illnesses for years on end. Those with bolder, thicker lines, though physically much stronger, seem to expend their energies in short bursts and find it harder to maintain their strength over a long period of time.

The empty hand

These people are more effective at controlling emotion and focusing their energies on the job in hand. Unless there are contradictory features, such as a very steeply curved Head line, they rarely waste time fretting, but the detachment they feel from their own nervous system means they may lack some sensitivity towards others.

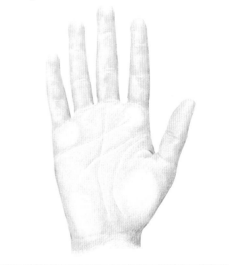

The full hand

This denotes a highly strung, very emotional worrier who lives on their nerves, scatters their energies about willy-nilly, and is aware of every little change in their bodies and surroundings. A very full hand denotes a highly complex person who is open to suggestion and possibly prone to psychosomatic disorders. If the palm is also markedly curved and juts out just beneath the little finger, its owner possesses a fidgety, highly charged mind that does not easily switch off. Relaxation techniques such as yoga will work wonders here.

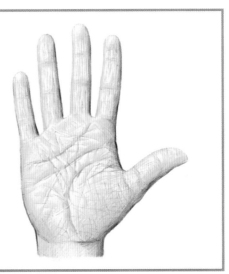

Part Three

Positive Action

Treating Common Ailments

So, you have mastered the basics of hand-reading, and identified the specific health indicators present in the hands. Armed with this information, you can now take positive action using the practical complementary health suggestions included in this section. Covering a wide range of common ailments – as well as offering ways to improve overall well-being and vitality – this section really does allow you to take your health into your own hands. Here, you will find a visual recap of the typical markings that are associated with specific conditions, together with their common symptoms and suggested therapies for general relief and prevention. 'Quick-fix' remedies are also given, for rapid relief. The appendix at the back of the book provides a quick-reference summary of each of the therapies referred to in this section. Remember that although you can certainly take charge of your own health, you must treat your findings with caution. Always consult a doctor if you are at all concerned about any aspect of your health.

Taking Your Health in Your Hands

Exercise caution

Supplements, remedies and techniques outlined in this book are suggested as a reference source only, not as a medical guide. Herbs, for example, contain active powerful properties even in minute doses, while certain types of massage may sometimes be counterproductive – some reflexology should not be practised on pregnant women, for example. To follow any therapy, consult your doctor before you begin. With vitamins and minerals, always take the daily recommended international units.

Tissue salts: abbreviations

1	Calc. Fluor.	Calcium Fluoride	6	Kali. Phos.	Potassium Phosphate
2	Calc. Phos.	Calcium Phosphate	7	Kali. Sulph.	Potassium Sulphate
3	Calc. Sulph.	Calcium Sulphate	8	Mag. Phos.	Magnesium Phosphate
4	Ferr. Phos.	Phosphate of Iron	9	Nat. Mur.	Sodium Chloride
5	Kali. Mur.	Potassium Chloride	10	Nat. Phos.	Sodium Phosphate
			11	Nat. Sulph.	Sodium Sulphate
			12	Silica	Silicic Oxide

Conditions of the senses

Eye problems

Look for ...

1 A large island in the Heart line beneath the ring finger is a classic symptom, but be aware that this may also represent heart or circulatory problems.

2 An island in the Head line beneath the mount of Apollo.

3 Some practitioners claim that a circular or semi-circular marking either above the Heart line beneath the ring finger, or attached to the inside edge of the Life line, shows susceptibility to cataracts.

Taking action

• Vitamin A is essential for healthy eyes.

• Eyebright, taken internally as an infusion or made into a lotion or compress and applied to the eyes is

Bates' theory

Try the following Bates exercise to promote good sight (see also Appendix, page 140). Make an effort every so often, when looking at an object, to shift your gaze from one side to the other and up and down. This works best when the shift is a small one and your eyes are relaxed.

a traditional remedy for weak or diseased eyes, and is said to boost sight.

• Carrot and bilberry capsules are recommended for night blindness.

• Silica for the treatment of sties; Kali. Phos. for weakness; Nat. Mur. for watery eyes; Ferr. Phos. for pain, inflammation and redness.

Hearing problems

Look for ...

A classic sign is an island in the Heart line below the middle finger.

Taking action

- Kali. Mur. and Ferr. Phos. tissue salts.
- Ginkgo Biloba has been found to help tinnitus (ringing in the ears).
- Ginger can be used to treat vertigo.
- Acupressure and acupuncture are useful for motion sickness, tinnitus and dizziness. Acupuncture bracelets, in particular, can help to stave off the worst effects of travel sickness.

Common symptoms and illnesses related to the senses

Symptoms Dizzy spells, motion sickness, ringing in the ears, nausea, loss of balance, earache, sties, poor general vision, poor night vision, blurred vision, difficulty reading, difficulty driving, loss of hearing

Illnesses Tinnitus, glue ear, cataracts, blindness, conjunctivitis, otitis, deafness, blepharitis, myopia or glaucoma

Reading the main signs: the senses

Look for clues in the line structure, especially in irregular formations in the Head or Heart lines.

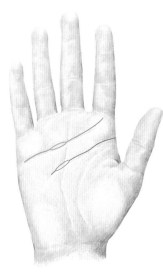

▲ Islands in the Head and Heart lines that occur beneath the ring finger may denote different eye problems.

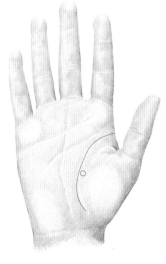

▲ A circular formation inside the Life line may denote susceptibility to cataracts.

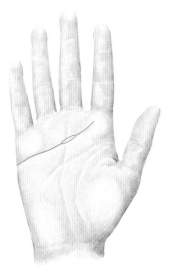

▲ An island in the Heart line directly beneath the middle finger may denote hearing difficulties or other ear problems.

Modern medical findings

These are early days in scientific research, but already we are seeing some very exciting results that seem to correlate both physical and psychological characteristics with the shape, construction and markings in the hand.

Foetal programming

During pregnancy, the foetus is immersed in a hormonal 'bath', the particular mix of which will influence how that foetus develops. Researchers are beginning to recognize that, because our hands are formed at the same time as the brain, testes/ovaries and heart – a critical time of foetal development – the same hormones that programme these organs will also be programming the hands in a similar manner. These pioneering findings mean that our hand-markings must act as a record of the pregnancy and also mirror our predisposition to disease.

Apples and pears

Research on body shapes suggests that people who tend to accumulate fat around the waist (called an apple body shape) have a shorter life expectancy than those who tend to put on weight around their hips and thighs (called a pear body shape).

The US National Center for Chronic Disease Prevention has discovered a correspondence between these types and the ridge count on our third and fourth fingers. Most people have just a few more ridges on their third (ring) finger than their fourth (little) finger. Those with little difference between the two tend to be pear-shaped, but those with twenty or more ridges on their ring fingers as compared to the little digit, tend towards the apple shape.

Since apple-shaped individuals are more prone to diabetes and heart disease, a ridge-difference test might prove a quick and inexpensive way to detect those who are at risk of developing these conditions.

Sex and creativity

A study reported in the journal, *Human Reproduction*, found that men whose right hands were not exact mirror images of their left ones tended to have a lower sperm count than those whose two hands matched each other perfectly.

Recent studies by a team from the UK's University of Liverpool have discovered a link between the relative lengths of the ring and index fingers in a man's hand and his levels of the sex hormone, testosterone. Those whose ring fingers were appreciably longer than their indexes had higher testosterone levels, leading to an increase in sex drive (the same team found that musicians tended to have much longer ring fingers than forefingers).

Mapping your health

All kinds of new and exciting scientific findings are now coming to light linking the hands and health, so perhaps it is only a matter of time before medical hand analysis is accepted in the doctor's surgery as an aid to diagnosis. However, it is slow work and a good deal more needs to be done. To summarize some of the findings made so far, I propose the 'map' of hand–health correspondences, opposite.

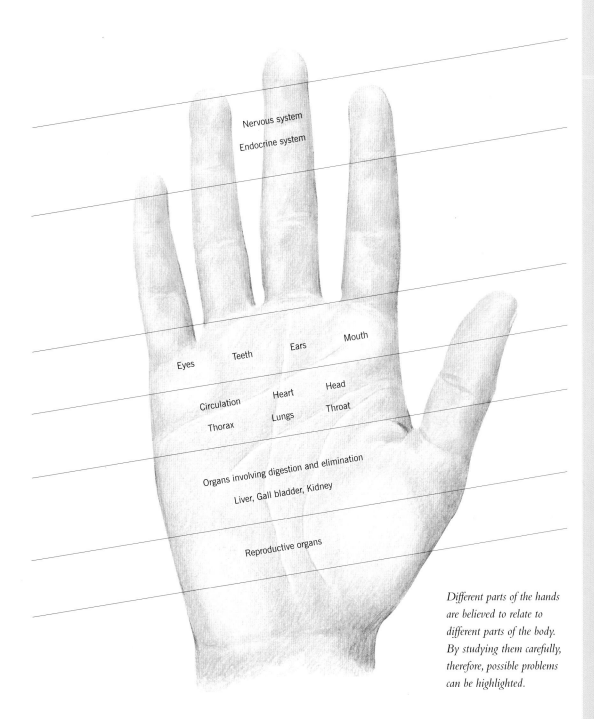

Nervous system

Endocrine system

Mouth

Ears

Teeth

Eyes

Head

Heart

Circulation

Throat

Thorax

Lungs

Organs involving digestion and elimination

Liver, Gall bladder, Kidney

Reproductive organs

*Different parts of the hands
are believed to relate to
different parts of the body.
By studying them carefully,
therefore, possible problems
can be highlighted.*

Conditions of the chest

Respiratory problems

A large category of disorders comprising sore throat, bronchitis, pneumonia, tuberculosis and lung disease.

Look for ...

1 Islands at the beginning of the Head line may register a predisposition to respiratory problems.
2 Nails curving around the tip of the finger. This usually starts with the nail on the left index finger, followed by the right, the left middle finger then the right one, and subsequently the rest of the digits.

3 More severe cases are marked by the humped nail.
4 With some serious respiratory conditions, the fingertips may swell and take on a 'clubbed' appearance (this may also occur with heart disease and severe circulatory problems).
5 Also in advanced cases, cyanosis (blue coloration) may tinge the nails and skin (also associated with certain cardiovascular problems).

Taking action

• Of the tissue salts, Kali Mur is said to ease congestion and sore throats. Preparation Q, a combination of Ferr. Phos., Kali. Mur., Kali. Phos. and Nat. Mur.,

Reading the main signs: the chest

Depending on the severity of the conditions, warning markings range from islands in the lines, through malformations of the nails to a blue discoloration (in severe cases, in both the skin tone and colour of the nail bed).

Islands at the beginning of ▷ the Head or Life lines denote a predisposition to respiratory problems, or childhood respiratory ailments.

▲ Blue discoloration of the skin, and even nail beds, can denote serious chest problems.

▲ Where both respiratory and heart disorders are present, fingertips may take on a clubbed appearance.

▲ Nails that are humped, or that curve around the fingertip, indicate that the lungs are under stress.

is recommended for catarrh and sinus problems.

- Infusions made with thyme and elecampane are thought to relax muscular spasms and have an expectorant action. Coltsfoot and white horehound teas are recommended for coughs and colds.
- Ephedra (which gives its name to ephedrine, a drug prescribed for problems with the respiratory tract) and plantain are also used for asthmatic and bronchial conditions.
- Current thinking suggests that dairy products may trigger respiratory problems, since they exacerbate the production of mucus and phlegm.

Quick fixes

For a blocked-up nose, try sprinkling a few drops of lavender, eucalyptus or sandalwood essential oil onto a tissue and leaving it on your desk or bedside table. In winter, sprinkle onto a wad of cotton wool and leave on top of a radiator so that the warmth releases the relaxing, antiseptic properties and aids sleep (do not do this on open-top heaters).

Common respiratory-related symptoms and illnesses

Symptoms Cough, tightness of the chest, congestion, wheezing, sneezing, runny nose, catarrh, fever, headache

Illnesses Common cold, influenza, sinusitis, asthma, bronchitis, pneumonia, lung disease, tuberculosis

---

Conditions of the stomach and abdomen

Acidity

Acidity may be a part of faulty digestion or a slow build-up in the system. Common causes are faulty diet and stress.

Look for ...

1 Flaring (fine lines like tongues of fire) running obliquely from the centre of the palm up towards the third and fourth fingers.
2 Veiling on the percussion edge – numerous fine, crisscrossing lines that cut across the ridge pattern on the part of the percussion beneath the beginning of the Heart line. Believed to represent a slow build-up of uric acid, which could also aggravate certain rheumatic conditions.

Taking action

- Phos. and Nat. Mur. tissue salts. Silica is helpful in eliminating chronic acidity but is a very slow worker.
- Mint tea, plus centaury and yarrow, all aid the digestive processes.
- Acidophilus, found in 'live' yogurt and in supplement form, is a type of bacteria that helps to maintain the balance of 'friendly' bacteria in the gut, easing digestion and helping to combat acidity.

Digestive problems

This category includes various disorders of the alimentary canal, stomach and intestines.

Look for ...

1 Fine flaring lines, rising obliquely from the centre of the palm towards the ring finger, suggest a tendency to intestinal overactivity.
2 A Luna mount that is heavily marked by lines can also signal intestinal problems.
3 Flabbiness of the basal phalanx of the index finger can denote a tendency to dyspepsia, mainly due to faulty nutrition.
4 Disorders of the gall bladder may be indicated by a triangular or diamond-shaped group of lines that are attached to the Life line, two-thirds of the way down the palm.
5 A fragmented Health line may denote stomach and intestinal disorders.

Taking action

• A vast range of herbal teas and preparations can aid digestion: peppermint for indigestion, nausea and stomach pain; thyme and balm mint for stomach cramps and diarrhoea; fennel for colic; dandelion as a blood-purifier; ginger and pineapple for indigestion, difficulty in digesting food, nausea and poor appetite.

• Two major groups of tissue salts are held in high regard here. Combination C, consisting of Mag. Phos., Nat. Phos., Nat. Sulph. and Silica, for all conditions involving acidity, heartburn and indigestion. And Combination S, comprising Kali. Mur., Nat. Phos. and Nat. Sulph., for treating acute stomach upsets, nausea and biliousness.

Hernia

A tendency to a hernia may be marked by a diamond or triangular-shaped formation of lines attached to the Life line about two-thirds of the way down the palm.

Obesity

Look for ...

1 Soft, plump basal phalanges on all the fingers is a sign of a sensual, self-indulgent and often indolent individual – such people are commonly overweight.
2 Little fat pads on the basal phalanges on the backs of the fingers mean a more long-term weight problem that has probably been building up since childhood and will be more difficult to shift.

Common symptoms and illnesses related to the stomach and abdomen

Symptoms Bloating, cramps, fatigue, constipation, diarrhoea, nausea, gas, stomach ache, skin rash, loss of appetite, fluid retention, heartburn, stomach inflammation, vomiting

Illnesses Acid reflux, rickets, irritable bowel syndrome, colitis, coeliac disease, diverticular disease, bowel cancer, Crohn's disease, appendicitis, food poisoning, gastritis, gallstones, anorexia nervosa, bulimia nervosa, peptic ulcers, malnutrition, diabetes

Taking action

- Willpower, exercise and a carefully calorie-controlled diet are the best ways of losing weight. Crash diets are not recommended, as these set up nutritional deficiencies and imbalances in the system. Those who are very overweight should always check with their doctors before undertaking any weight-loss programmes.
- Some herbalists maintain that green tea, guarana and bean husk aid weight-loss. Pineapple preparations are reputed to act against cellulitis.
- Those who acknowledge the role of the Moon's energies in our lives claim that targeting your calorie-control regime to commence after the Full Moon, taking advantage of the decreasing lunar power, may trigger weight loss faster and give you the incentive you need to persevere until you reach your desired goal.

Reading the main signs: the stomach and abdomen

A pale hand whose palm has a flabby or doughy feel is a first sign of irregularities.

◀ A triangular or diamond formation attached to the outside of the Life line may signal a hernia (although it may also point to other conditions).

▲ A doughy hand with very full basal phalanges is a mark of obesity.

▲ A pasty-looking hand is a sign of stomach problems.

◀ Fine lines in a horizontal patch on the percussion edge, or obliquely through the centre of the palm, point to an acid/alkaline imbalance, which can lead to digestive problems.

Massage for the hands

The hand is a perfect part of the body to massage. It is easy to massage your own hands, and you can do so unobtrusively, almost anywhere. You can use a combination of different techniques – from reflexology (see pages 136–7), aromatherapy and acupressure to effleurage and deep-pressure massage.

Effleurage
This is the main technique used for a general toning of the system (see below), stroking either with the whole hand or the thumb.

A light stroke has a relaxing effect, while more pressure stimulates the circulation, muscles and tissues. Massage is always performed upwards, towards the heart. Even if working from the wrist down to the fingers, sweep movements up in the direction of the arm and allow the massaging hand to trail lightly back down, drawing out through the fingers.

Use one hand to massage your other one, using both heel and thumb to apply pressure, and giving extended manipulation to tender spots. A lubricant is not essential, but scented

Body toning hand massage

Follow these simple steps to give your hand a good workout.

1 Starting at the wrist, press your thumb tip in light circular movements, horizontally across the wrist and over onto the back of the arm. This helps to loosen muscles and ligaments at the wrist.

2 Press the heel of one hand against the knuckles of the other so as to push the hand down perpendicularly to the wrist. Holding the arm outstretched and palm upwards, grasp the fingers and pull them downwards until you feel tension at the wrist. Repeat in the same way for the other hand.

3 With the palm of one hand resting on the backs of the fingers of the other, massage the back of the hand by pressing the thumb tip up between the tendons. Start with the webbing between the thumb and index finger, first pushing upwards, then allowing the thumb action to trail lightly backwards. Repeat for all fingers, then do the other hand.

talcum powder or aromatherapy oils (always dilute these in a carrier oil) are pleasant and often therapeutic. None of the movements should be forced, especially if there is the slightest resistance, or if injury or disease will not permit.

Health notes

Whether massage is conducted by yourself or by another, hands should always be washed at the end of the routine.

Beneficial aromatherapy massage oils

- Neroli (from the flowers of the bitter orange tree) – calms nervous conditions
- Bergamot – antiseptic tonic
- Rosemary – stimulant, especially beneficial in memory loss
- Black pepper – aids concentration
- Ylang Ylang – aphrodisiac

Oils are potent and can produce adverse reactions, especially if pregnant – check for contraindications.

4 Firmly pinch the four webs between each of your digits in turn for several seconds at a time, applying a circular motion between thumb and index finger. This breaks down toxins that gather in the webbing, ready to be eliminated by your body's natural cleansing mechanisms. Repeat in the same way for the other hand.

5 Turn the hand over to work on the palm side. Starting at the base of the palm, make small circular movements with the thumb, working across the palm. Start from the thumb edge and work across the palm, section by section, to the percussion edge. Return to any tender spots for several seconds at a time. Repeat for the other hand.

6 Starting with the thumb tip, apply the same circular movements all the way down each digit in turn, pinching and rubbing the joints en route. This reaches major acupressure points located in the fingers and thumbs. Repeat on the other hand.

7 Interlace the fingers and stretch each hand against the other, feeling the pull at the base of your fingers. Shake your hands vigorously until they tingle.

Conditions of the immune system

AIDS

Not enough research has as yet been carried
out to be able to put together a list of markings
for this illness. Observations to date, however,
have included fragmented skin ridges, which
are already associated with a vulnerable
immune system.

Reading the main signs: the immune system

Research continues into changes in the
ridge formations in the palm that may show
a link with more serious immune disorders,
although no conclusive results have been
reached to date.

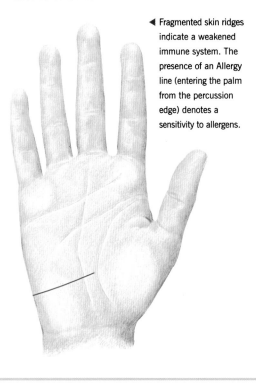

◀ Fragmented skin ridges
indicate a weakened
immune system. The
presence of an Allergy
line (entering the palm
from the percussion
edge) denotes a
sensitivity to allergens.

Common allergy-related symptoms and illnesses

Symptoms Rash, shock, breathing difficulties, stiff
joints, lethargy, disturbed sleep, fainting

Illnesses Hay fever, psoriasis, osteoarthritis, gout, ME

Allergies

The major general marking here is the Allergy
line, lying horizontally across the mount of
Luna. This just shows a general problem,
however, and is not allergen-specific.

- Check for stress markings in the hand, as some
  allergies are stress-related.
- Keeping records of diet, contact with chemicals
  and so on, plus any adverse reactions, may isolate
  particular allergens.
- Vitamin C and garlic may help.

Immune system weakness

Look for ...
Fragmented skin ridges.

Taking action
- Mistletoe, though toxic in the wild, is said to
  strengthen the immune system when prepared
  specially by a professional practitioner.
- Echinacea has produced excellent results in building
  up the immune system and even aiding people who
  are suffering from ME.

Conditions of the glands

Thyroid imbalance

Problems with the thyroid gland occur when it malfunctions and becomes overactive or underactive, producing too much or too little thyroxine. Both conditions have serious implications for growth and metabolism. Symptoms of overactivity include hyperactivity, nervous tension, rapid heart action, weight loss, clammy hands and a slight finger tremor. With underactivity there is unusual weight gain, lethargy, aching muscles and cold, dry hands.

Look for ...

The thyroid gland is believed to correspond to the tip of the little finger, and vertical lines here are thought to show a stressed gland, but do not distinguish between under- and overactivity. However, there are symptoms linked with either one or the other.

Overactive or hyperthyroidism

1 A fine finger tremor when the hands are outstretched.
2 Smooth skin with a satin sheen.
3 Nails with markedly heavy vertical ridging.

Common symptoms and illnesses related to thyroid problems

Symptoms Hyperactivity or lethargy, rapid heart action, weight loss, bulging eyes, enlargement at the front of the neck, fatigue, sudden changes in weight, nervous tension, tremor, aching muscles, cold/dry hands.

Illnesses Hypothyroidism or hyperthyroidism

---

4 Very large moons in the nails.
5 Damp, clammy hands.

Underactive or hypothyroidism

1 Dry, cold, rough hands.
2 Concave or 'spoon' nails.
3 Nails lacking all moons.
4 Brittle nails that split or break easily.

Taking action

• Iodine in kelp or seaweed tablets.
• Calcium iodide.

Reading the main signs: the thyroid gland

The fingertips are believed to be linked to the endocrine system, with each finger corresponding to a particular gland.

Concave nails may indicate ▶ hypothyroidism.

▲ Nails with heavy vertical ridges may indicate hyperthyroidism.

▲ A cluster of fine vertical lines running down the tip of the little finger denotes a tendency to thyroid problems.

Conditions of the sexual organs

Reproductive system disorders

Look for ...

1 A diamond or triangular formation of lines attached to the Life line about a third of the way up from the palm.

2 A star formation at the point where the Head and Health lines intersect.

3 A bracelet at the wrist that markedly humps up onto the palm is a sign of potential problems in childbirth.

4 A fine tracery of lines that covers the base of the mount of Luna.

5 A fine chaining of the Head and Heart lines can suggest a sodium/potassium imbalance, which may contribute to PMS.

Taking action

• Sage is a key herb for PMS, painful and irregular menstruation, and general menopausal problems; hops and alfalfa for hormonal regulation; motherwort and camomile for their soothing properties; shepherd's purse to guard against internal haemorrhaging, especially of the uterus.

• Because this category covers a wide range of disorders, there is an equally wide variety of biochemical remedies. Combination N, however, comprising Calc. Phos., Kali. Mur., Kali. Phos. and Mag. Phos., is recommended for painful periods and allied gynaecological problems.

• Calcium sulphate may aid impotency.

• Oil of evening primrose is believed to have some

Reading the main signs: The sexual/reproductive organs

Indications of potential problems may be found mainly in subsidiary markings attached to the main lines, or in a noticeable displacement of one or more lines.

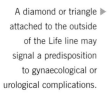

A diamond or triangle ▷ attached to the outside of the Life line may signal a predisposition to gynaecological or urological complications.

◁ A star where Head and Health lines meet, or a skewed top rascette that humps up into the palm, may suggest problems with reproduction, fertility or childbirth.

effect on regularizing the menstrual cycle.
- Of the Bach Flower Remedies, 'Walnut' is especially beneficial when adjusting to transitions such as puberty and the menopause.

Quick fixes

Exercises that keep a woman's pelvic floor muscles well toned and flexible help prevent embarrassing stress incontinence, avoid painful prolapse of the uterus, and increase pleasure during lovemaking (these muscles become especially slack after childbirth). Daily exercises can be done quickly anywhere – while waiting in line for a bus, for example! Simply squeeze the muscles, hold for a few minutes and relax. Another useful exercise involves stopping mid-flow when urinating, and holding for a few seconds before continuing again.

Common symptoms and illnesses related to problems of the reproductive organs

Symptoms Tender, painful breasts, cessation of menstruation, irregular bleeding, vaginal discharge, shock, fever, mood swings, lumps, impotence

Illnesses Fibroids, pelvic inflammatory disease, endometriosis, toxic shock, prolapse of the uterus, infertility, vaginitis, PMS, ectopic pregnancy, hydrocele (male urogenital problem), variocele (ditto), orchitis (inflamed testicles), epididymal cysts, cancer, AIDS

Conditions of the liver, kidneys and bladder

Liver dysfunction

Look for …

1 Yellowish tinge to the skin on the hands and the nails.
2 A broken Health line.

Taking action

- Fumitory stimulates the secretion of bile; liverwort purifies the blood; centaury relieves pain in the liver and spleen; dandelion tones up a sluggish liver.
- Nat. Sulph. is recommended in disorders of the liver and gall bladder, and Kali. Sulph. in boosting a sluggish liver.

Quick fixes

Drinking a glass of warm water with some freshly squeezed lemon juice first thing in the morning gets your system, especially the liver, off to a good start.

Urinary problems

These include kidney and bladder disorders.

Look for …

1 A Luna mount cross-hatched with fine lines.
2 A yellowish scarring or small, callus-like cluster of hard skin close to the outer side of the Life line.
3 A vertical line down the side of Mercury mount.

(*Continued on page 122*)

The four hand types

Here is a health profile and treatment guide for the four main hand types.

Earth hand

Avoid:

- stress produced by erratic routines
- nervous tension
- weight gain
- physical indolence and self-indulgence
- negative attitudes

Encourage:

- exercise and fresh air
- outdoor interests
- regularized lifestyle
- good sleep patterns
- positive attitude
- healthy diet

Taking action

Calcium is the mineral associated with the Earth hand, essential for many health aspects, from strong teeth and bones to effective blood clotting and good muscle tone.

- Among the tissue salts: Calc. Fluor., Calc. Phos., Calc. Sulph. Other mineral supplements include Calcium ascorbate, which combines Vitamin C for easy absorption, Calcium aspartate and Calcium gluconate.
- Kelp is a rich source of calcium; so too are dairy products, almonds, and sardines and whitebait (where the bones are also eaten).
- Magnesium and Vitamin D assist the absorption and deployment of calcium.
- Violet, rose, grapes, willow and comfrey are all associated with the Earth category.

Air hand

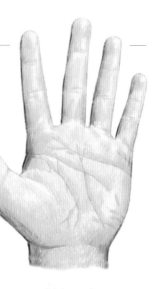

Avoid:

- being stuck in a rut
- too many irons in the fire
- nervous tension
- mental exhaustion

Encourage:

- healthy exchange of news and views
- flexible routines
- intellectual activities
- regular physical exercise

Taking action

Because of the incessant demands on their mental and nervous systems, Air-handed folk do well to think about magnesium – the great nerve-relaxer – when they are feeling run-down.

- Among the tissue salts, Mag. Phos. is the nerve restorative. Other mineral supplements include Magnesium ascorbate, which combines with Vitamin C for easy absorption, Magnesium aspartate and Magnesium gluconate.
- Kelp is a good source of magnesium, as are nuts and grains.
- Lavender, marjoram, mint, ash and elderflower are both associated with the Air category.

Fire hand

Avoid:

- mental or physical overload
- overly rich or spicy food
- too much alcohol or other stimulants
- sudden, dramatic moods
- rushing around and careless, precipitate action that can lead to accidents
- leaving things to the last minute
- restlessness
- putting on weight

Encourage:

- peace and harmony (yoga, for instance)
- regular workouts into which energies can be channelled
- keeping an even pace at home and work

Taking action

Potassium is the mineral particularly associated with the physically and mentally active Fire type, as it keeps muscles toned and feeds the nerves.

- Among the tissue salts: Kali. Mur., Kali. Phos. and Kali. Sulph. Also Potassium gluconate and Potassium aspartate.
- Fish and kelp are rich sources of potassium, as are bananas, raisins, dates, avocados, carrots, cabbage and spinach.
- Peppermint tea, hops, onions, leeks, rosemary, sage, dandelion and borage are all associated with the Fire category.

Water hand

Avoid:

- stress through competition
- mood swings, especially melancholia
- repressing emotions
- irrational or over-imaginative fears
- escapism through drugs or alcohol
- negativity

Encourage:

- expression of feelings
- peace and harmony at home and work
- confidence through developing one's talents
- a rational approach to problems
- gentle sports such as swimming
- balance and moderation

Taking action

Because of its associations with water, sodium is the mineral here, responsible for maintaining the body's water balance. However, Sodium chloride, in the form of table salt, is all too prevalent in the Western diet, so a reduction, rather than a supplement, is perhaps advisable nowadays.

Sodium is also essential for: the digestive process; neutralizing acid, which can help to prevent rheumatic conditions; regulating glandular and nerve functioning. This helps Water types because they are prone to digestive upsets, rheumatism, headaches, nausea, apathy and despondency, watery eyes and allergies.

- Tissue salts: Nat. Mur., Nat. Phos. and Nat. Sulph.
- Sodium deficiency is now rare in the West, but foods with a high concentration include cheeses and green olives.
- Verbena, tarragon, witch hazel and geranium are all associated with the Water category.

Taking action

- Infection of the kidneys can cause serious long-term damage. If suspected, consult a doctor immediately.
- Dandelion and stinging nettle are both herbal diuretics used to flush out the system; rupture-wort eases inflammation of the urinary tract; bladderwort has been used as a remedy for bladder disorders.
- Of the tissue salts, Ferr. Phos., Nat. Mur. and Mag. Phos. for stress incontinence; these three again, together with Kali. Phos. and Kali. Mur., for the treatment of cystitis; Calc. Phos., to prevent any bed-wetting.
- Live yoghurt, eaten or applied to the external areas, will help relieve and cool the irritation that accompanies thrush and redress the balance of healthy bacteria that helps prevent the condition.
- Cranberry juice, taken several times a day, will help to de-acidify the urinary tract and ease many bladder or urinary discomforts.

Common symptoms and illnesses related to problems of the eliminatory organs

Symptoms Pain or blood when passing water, yellowing of skin or eyes, abdominal pain, nausea, incontinence, excessive thirst, frequent urination, fluid retention

Illnesses Cystitis, Bright's disease, hepatitis, jaundice, gallstones, nephritis, diabetes, cirrhosis

Reading the main signs: the eliminatory organs

A yellowing that has nothing to do with ethnic skin tone or tanning, together with marked yellow nail beds, point to liver dysfunction.

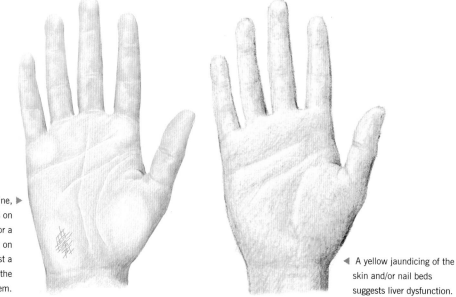

A cluster of fine, ▶ cross-hatched lines on the Luna mount, or a tiny, wart-like growth on the palm, both suggest a potential problem of the urinary system.

◀ A yellow jaundicing of the skin and/or nail beds suggests liver dysfunction.

Conditions of the heart and blood

Anaemia

Look for ...

1 A pale or even white skin on the hands is a first clue.
2 When fingers are flexed backwards, the lines look pale or even run to white. Exposure to chemicals may also be responsible for this, so eliminate this cause first. Lines may look pale after menstruation, when iron has been lost in the menstrual flow.

Taking action

- If feeling washed out following a period, try to avoid reaching for the iron pills (unless medically prescribed), as these can upset your stomach and intestines. Consider, instead, boosting the blood by taking the following:
- Iron-rich foods such as green-leaf vegetables, liver, molasses, fish and shellfish, raisins and nuts.
- Vitamin B complex, particularly B12.
- Vitamin C to aid iron absorption.
- Vegans are especially prone to iron deficiency because their diet excludes both meat and dairy products. Increasing their intake of soya-based products, molasses, dried fruit and green-leaf vegetables should help restore the balance.
- Calc. Phos. and the Ferr. Phos tissue salts.
- Herbally, try alfalfa and nettle.

Heart and circulatory problems

These problems are many and varied, from high blood pressure, through angina and arteriosclerosis/atherosclerosis (hardening of arteries), to heart disease. Disorders may be genetic or congenital in origin (often revealed by abnormalities in skin-ridge patterns) or can be caused by poor diet, lifestyle, environmental factors or the general wear and tear of ageing. Many hand-markings show a tendency to cardiovascular problems.

Look for ...

Indicators include:

1 Short, often triangular or shell-shaped nails – a susceptibility to high blood pressure.
2 Skin indicators include possessing a larger than average number of fingertip whorl patterns and having an axial triradius pattern that is displaced high up on the percussion edge towards the Heart line.
3 Heart line features include: a line that is chained for much of its course; a single weak, thin line with no feathering, islanding or chaining where it enters the palm at the percussion edge; a marked break; a star over the line (this may indicate stroke); two long branches shooting out of the line and descending down into the mount of Luna (also possible stroke indicator); a single large blue island in the line below the ring or little fingers. Little hard nodules may develop around the Heart line beneath the ring finger immediately prior to, or following, a heart attack.
4 A star on the Head line (possibility of stroke).
5 Bulbous or clubbed fingertips.
6 Blue discoloration of nails and skin.
7 The Simian line suggests a genetic or congenital predisposition.
8 A ring fingertip heavily marked with vertical lines – possible high blood pressure.
9 Very red hands or unnaturally red lines – possible high blood pressure.
10 Cold hands and fingers point to poor circulation.
11 Horizontal white lines across the nails are associated with heart disease.
12 A predominant mount of Jupiter always suggests a large appetite for rich foods and strong drink – which often causes heart problems.

Taking action

Following a good diet, especially cutting out salt and reducing alcohol intake, taking exercise, possible weight reduction and giving up smoking, are essential for maintaining good circulation and a healthy heart. Research suggests that regular intake of the following helps to keep the heart healthy and may prevent the onset of disease:

- Daily garlic tablets or garlic in the diet is said to lower high blood pressure.
- Oily fish.
- GLA (Gamma Linolenic Acid), particularly concentrated in oil of evening primrose.
- Reduction of saturated fats and an increase of mono- or polyunsaturated fats.

- Herbally, broom is recommended for low blood pressure; bamboo gum for atherosclerosis; gugulon for high cholesterol; ginkgo to boost circulation.
- Kali. Phos., Calc. Phos. and Calc. Fluor. tissue salts are said to boost circulation.
- Silica, though slow-acting, is reputed to make arterial walls stronger and more elastic.
- Vitamin E, or tocopherol, seems to be help maintain healthy circulation and even blood pressure. But care must be taken by those with hypertension when they first start taking this vitamin, for it can have adverse effects if taken suddenly in too high a dosage. These people should begin with a very low dosage, no more than 100iu daily, and very, very slowly build up to no more than 400iu.

Reading the main signs: the heart and blood

A tendency to high blood pressure and heart disease is linked to an increased number of fingertip whorl patterns.

▼ A marked blue, red or white discoloration of the skin are clues to irregularities of the cardiovascular system.

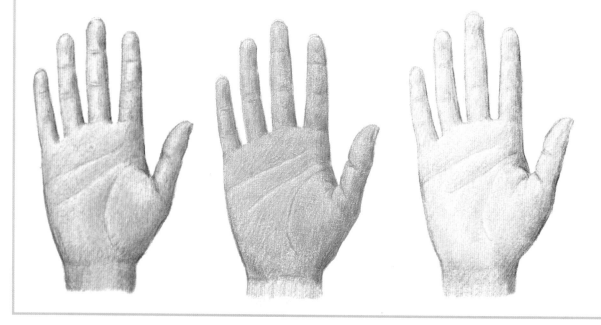

Common symptoms and illnesses related to circulatory problems

Symptoms Fatigue, dizziness, breathlessness, tingling sensations in the limbs, palpitations, excessive perspiration, headaches, tightening of the chest, heartburn, pain down the left side of the body

Illnesses Blood poisoning, high or low blood pressure, angina, arteriosclerosis, heart disease

Quick fixes

Studies have shown that meditation can help to reduce high blood pressure. Spending just fifteen minutes a day thinking calm thoughts can make a huge difference. Try to find a quiet place, sit comfortably and imagine, for example, that you are in a beautiful garden. Savour all the details, drop your shoulders, breathe rhythmically and feel all the cares of the world slipping away.

—·—·— Normal angle

—·—·— Angle may denote a problem

▲ A fan-shaped nail is a sign that the system is stressed.

▼ A poorly formed Heart line, or a star on the Head line beneath the ring finger, may indicate a problem with the heart or blood supply.

◀ Heart defects may be denoted by a skewed 'atd' angle of the triradius ridge patterns on the palm.

Homeopathy

Homeopathy is a therapeutic system that seeks to restore the body's harmony. Since the markings in the hand are excellent indicators of potential imbalance, this would seem an ideal therapy to use in conjunction with hand analysis, either as a preventive measure or as a restorative.

Like heals like

Homeopathy stimulates the body's innate forces of recovery and triggers it to heal itself. The term is taken from Greek words – *homoios* meaning 'like' and *patheia*, meaning 'disease' or 'suffering', and the system works on the principle that 'like heals like'. Essentially, what this means is that a substance which, when given to healthy individuals, produces particular symptoms may be given to help the recovery of a patient whose illness is displaying similar symptoms to those seen in healthy people. For example, we all know how stinging nettles produce itchy, burning skin. Interestingly, someone who is sick and whose illness presents itchy, blistering skin may be given homeopathically prepared Urtica urens (a decoction made from stinging nettles) as a remedy.

The practice of homeopathy is holistic, since it deals not just with symptoms and diseases, but with the whole person. Its remedies are sourced mainly from mineral and vegetable extracts, although some are based on specific metal and biological materials. The medicinal substances used are very, very highly diluted, yet, even in such minute doses, they can be highly effective, with rare side effects.

Origins

Although the principles of curing 'like with like' were recognized by Hippocrates, back in the fifth century BCE, the origins of the modern system go back to Dr Samuel Hahnemann, a German physician who lived and worked in the twentieth century. He discovered that when he took cinchona bark it produced malaria-type symptoms, which he found curious since cinchona (later known as quinine) was the very drug given to treat malaria.

Suggested remedies

Although there are several thousand homeopathic remedies, here are a few that a practising homeopath might suggest to counteract possible clinical conditions denoted by particular hand-markings. Note that the same remedy may be used for different ailments – essentially, homeopathic remedies treat the person not the disease.

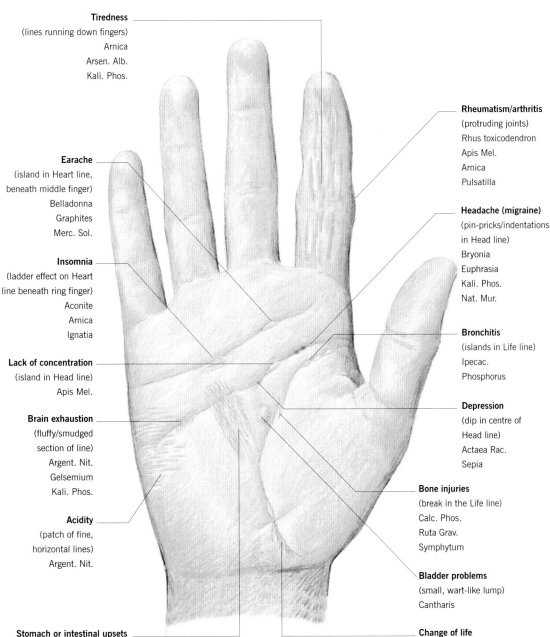

Tiredness
(lines running down fingers)
Arnica
Arsen. Alb.
Kali. Phos.

Earache
(island in Heart line,
beneath middle finger)
Belladonna
Graphites
Merc. Sol.

Insomnia
(ladder effect on Heart
line beneath ring finger)
Aconite
Arnica
Ignatia

Lack of concentration
(island in Head line)
Apis Mel.

Brain exhaustion
(fluffy/smudged
section of line)
Argent. Nit.
Gelsemium
Kali. Phos.

Acidity
(patch of fine,
horizontal lines)
Argent. Nit.

Stomach or intestinal upsets
(patch of fine lines running
obliquely through centre
of palm)
Carbo. Veg.
Arsen. Alb.

Rheumatism/arthritis
(protruding joints)
Rhus toxicodendron
Apis Mel.
Arnica
Pulsatilla

Headache (migraine)
(pin-pricks/indentations
in Head line)
Bryonia
Euphrasia
Kali. Phos.
Nat. Mur.

Bronchitis
(islands in Life line)
Ipecac.
Phosphorus

Depression
(dip in centre of
Head line)
Actaea Rac.
Sepia

Bone injuries
(break in the Life line)
Calc. Phos.
Ruta Grav.
Symphytum

Bladder problems
(small, wart-like lump)
Cantharis

Change of life
(island, bar or tasselled
branches on, over or
coming off Life line)
Pulsatilla
Sepia

Stress and conditions of the nervous system

Depression

This term covers a multitude of disorders, from serious mental disease to simply feeling down. Though it is quite natural to go through periods of ups and downs, and sometimes feeling downright miserable, true 'clinical' depression is a medical condition that can last for a long time and severely affect the lives of sufferers, and those they live with.

Look for ...

1 Islands in the Head line usually suggest times of worry, and anxiety that may well spark off a period of depression.
2 Perhaps one of the best indications of a bout of depression is seen by a dip in the Head line, from the apex of which shoots out a tiny, downswept branch.
3 A markedly curved Head line flowing deep into the mount of Luna suggests an overactive mentality where the imagination can sometimes run wild.
4 The 'full hand' reveals a tendency to hypersensitivity and neurotic moods.
5 A heavy trauma line cutting across the Life line and proceeding further up to cut through the other major lines as well. This represents a major upset which could potentially lead to depression. The deeper, the stronger and the longer the line, the more impact the traumatic event has upon its owner.
6 An over-developed Saturn mount is often a sign of a predisposition to depression, melancholia and also moodiness.
7 Deep lines that run up from the base of the fingers denote chronic tiredness which can all too often bring on a sense of despondency.
8 Horizontal lines across the tips of the fingers indicate personal problems. These may also confirm other markings of depression seen on the hand, and point to a root cause of the condition.
9 Vertical lines across the top phalanges of the fingers denote hormonal activity which may trigger serious mood swings.

Taking action

• Vitamin C.
• Amino acid complex.
• Magnesium and B6 (a deficiency may be a contributing factor in depression).
• Exposure to bright light for sufferers of SAD syndrome (Seasonal Affective Disorder).
• Californian poppy for its sedative properties; ginseng as a stimulant and tonic; a valerian infusion for hysteria, nervous exhaustion and agitation; infusion of borage, or its flowers, as a pick-me-up.
• Kali. Phos., Calc. Phos. and Nat. Mur. tissue salts.
• 'Gentian', 'Gorse' and 'Sweet Chestnut' Bach Flower Remedies.

Nervous disorders

This is a large catch-all category that includes all manner of nervousness, agitation, anxiety and neuroses.

Look for ...

1 A 'full hand', covered with lines.
2 A lean, oblong-shaped palm with long, lean fingers and a weak-looking thumb.
3 An over-developed, much-lined Mercury mount.
4 A bulge high on the percussion edge directly beneath the little finger signals an overactive, fretful mentality.
5 A long, curved Head line that slopes deeply into the mount of Luna denotes a highly imaginative temperament that may be prone to neurosis.
6 A series of fine horizontal lines cutting across the Life line shows an anxious personality.

7 The Simian line is associated with deep inner tension.

8 Wedge or fan-shaped nails, tapering towards the base.

Taking action

See suggestions under 'Depression' (left) plus:

- Yoga, meditation, relaxation, deep-breathing techniques, reflexology, acupuncture and aromatherapy may all calm the individual.
- Mag. Phos. and Kali. Phos. are recommended nerve restoratives.
- Soothing herbal teas such as camomile; passion flower, valerian and hops are other natural sedatives.
- Bach Flower Remedies 'Recovery Remedy'.

Sleep disorders

Look for ...

1 A tiny, ladder-like series of lines beneath the Heart line, roughly below the ring finger. This highlights that the sleep pattern is disturbed, and by implication may suggest that the nervous system is also under stress, too.

2 Vertical lines that travel up the two basal phalanges of the fingers.

Taking action

- Calcium, or a calcium/magnesium imbalance, may be at fault.
- Camomile tea taken before bed.
- Kali. Phos. may help if nervousness or excitability leads to restless sleep; Nat. Sulph. and Nat. Mur. can help when sleep is not refreshing.
- Milky drinks before bed help to induce more relaxed sleep.

Stress

Look for ...

1 Horizontal lines stretching across the fingertips. As each digit governs a specific aspect of our lives, a greater concentration of these 'white lines' on any particular finger will point to the underlying cause of the problem.

2 A single island in the Head line below the middle finger shows that its owner cannot cope with high pressure and should steer clear of experiencing over-demanding situations.

3 A 'fuzzy' section of Head line denotes a potentially stressful period when greater mental demands are put on the individual. The duration of this period can be timed on the line.

4 Long-term stress can cause the skin ridges to break up. This is easier to pick up on a print rather than with the naked eye. Such a break-up is a warning that the whole constitution is weakened and is now more vulnerable to disease. When the constitution is strengthened again, the ridges fairly rapidly re-knit themselves into their normal long, continuous lines.

Common stress-related symptoms and illnesses

Symptoms Anxiety, panic attacks, insomnia, tiredness, low energy, sweating, flushing, trembling, palpitations, diarrhoea, nausea, faintness, itchy skin, pins and needles, anger, irritability, addictions, low sex drive, depression

Illnesses Nervous tension, nervous breakdown, stomach upsets, stomach ulcers, headaches, migraine, skin complaints (psoriasis, eczema, rashes), sudden weight gain or loss, arthritis, poor circulation, high blood pressure, menstrual problems, chest pain

Taking action

- Kali. Phos. helps to relax the nervous system; Mag. Phos. relaxes tense nerves, especially if the stress produces headaches.
- Camomile tea is a great relaxant and soothing for the nerves, as are catmint, lemon balm and passion flower capsules.

Tiredness

Look for ...

1 Deep lines that run vertically up the two basal phalanges of the fingers.
2 A ladder-like series of little lines leading up to the Heart line beneath the ring finger shows that the sleep pattern is disturbed.
3 Lines that run white when the fingers are flexed

Quick fixes

If you are going out for the evening after a hard day's work and are feeling rather jaded, try sitting under a red-bulbed lamp for five minutes to recharge your batteries – make it an orange one if you suffer from high blood pressure.

back are a sign of iron-deficiency anaemia, a common cause of tiredness.

Taking action

- Mag. Phos., Ferr. Phos. and Kali. Phos. tissue salts.
- When iron deficiency is suspected, follow suggestions under 'Anaemia' (see page 123).
- 'Olive' Bach Flower Remedy.

Reading the main signs: the nervous system

Classic indications of a highly strung nervous condition is a palm that is covered in a cobweb of lines.

◀ A 'full hand' means that stress has reached crisis point.

Horizontal markings on ▶ the fingertips are among the earliest signs of stress.

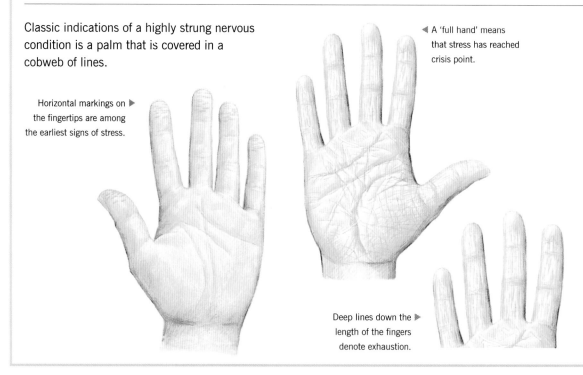

Deep lines down the ▶ length of the fingers denote exhaustion.

Memory loss

Many different conditions may impair the memory. Forgetful periods at any time of life are normal, especially during stressful times, but the most common cause is the slow erosion that comes with age.

Look for ...

Clinical memory loss, whether caused by injury or diseases of the brain or nervous system (such as dementia), may be registered on the hand by a thinning and fraying of the Head line towards its end. In some cases, the line may visibly wilt downwards towards the Luna mount and may appear as chained, feathered or even fragmented.

Taking action

- Minerals and tissue salt remedies include Zinc, Calc. Fluor. and Silica.
- Herbal preparations to boost memory and concentration include ginseng, schisandra and pollen capsules. The latter is especially recommended for the elderly.
- Psychological training which includes mnemonic techniques can help to improve retention and retrieval of information from memory.

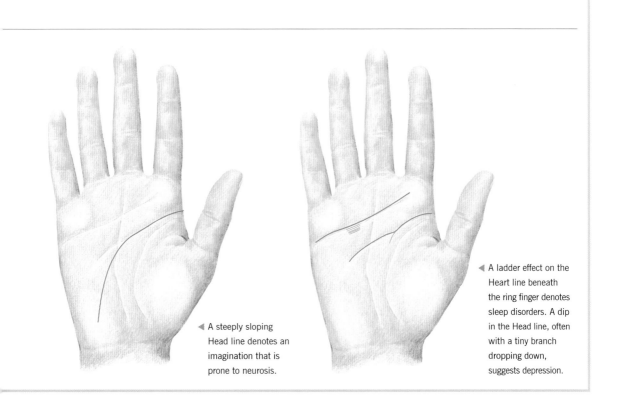

◀ A steeply sloping Head line denotes an imagination that is prone to neurosis.

◀ A ladder effect on the Heart line beneath the ring finger denotes sleep disorders. A dip in the Head line, often with a tiny branch dropping down, suggests depression.

Conditions of the joints, muscles and skeleton

Backache

Backache is a complex problem since different conditions may variously be due to injury, general wear and tear, pain referred from other areas altogether, congenital factors or even psychological problems (such as low self-esteem that can cause people to carry themselves in damaging ways).

Look for …
The main indication of back or spinal trouble is an island occurring halfway down the Life line.

Taking action
• B complex vitamins, Vitamin C and Calcium may aid some conditions.
• Of the tissue salts, Ferr. Phos. works on strains, sprains and muscle stiffness high in the neck. Use Combination G, comprising Calc. Fluor., Calc. Phos., Kali Phos. and Nat. Mur., for backache and lumbago.

Quick fixes

Try a yoga exercise called 'The Twist' to keep the spine supple while at the same time trimming the waistline. Sit on the floor with your back straight, feet together and legs stretched out in front of you. Place your left hand firmly on the floor behind you and let that take your weight. Bring your right leg up and over your left leg, placing your right foot on the floor next to your left knee. Now, twist your body as far around to the left as you can, so you are looking over your left shoulder. Hold for a count of ten, then straighten up and repeat on the other side.

Rheumatic diseases

These include rheumatism, gout, osteoarthritis and also rheumatoid arthritis. The main characteristic of these ailments is painful inflammation, sometimes serious distortion, of joints such as knuckles.

Look for …
1 Swollen joints. In the more crippling form of rheumatoid arthritis, the knuckles may be misshapen and the fingers badly distorted.
2 An early sign of a predisposition to rheumatism in general may be seen by veiling (a dense cluster of fine lines cutting through the skin-ridge pattern) on the percussion edge. When they occur on the percussion edge just below the Heart line, they suggest the build-up of acidity that may be implicated in triggering and aggravating rheumatic conditions.
3 Heavy vertical ridging of the nails.
4 Very full basal phalanges show that the diet is faulty, which could be a contributory factor. If the base of the index finger is particularly large, it may be illustrating a predisposition to rheumatic problems.
5 A large Luna mount that is heavily marked with many lines.

Taking action
• Silica and Nat. Phos. tissue salts.
• Cod liver oil.
• Vitamin C.
• Many herbal preparations have anti-inflammatory properties and so can benefit these conditions.
• Devil's claw and bamboo gum help to relieve joint pain and restore some mobility.
• Change in diet if all basal phalanges are very podgy.

Common symptoms and illnesses related to the bones and joints

Symptoms Pain or stiffness in the joints, swellings and inflammation, heat sensation in the joints, painful tendons, trapped nerve, distortion of the fingers, brittle bones

Illnesses Slipped disc, sciatica, fibromyalgia, osteoporosis, osteoarthritis, rheumatoid arthritis, ME

Reading the main signs: the joints and skeleton

Obvious rheumatic damage is seen in inflamed knuckles. In severe cases, the fingers distort and lose mobility.

▼ An island on the Life line denotes back or spinal weakness. A clean break in this line may suggest injury leading to a broken bone.

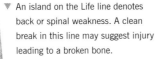

▲ Heavily ridged nails often accompany rheumatic diseases.

A cluster of fine lines on the edge of ▶ the palm denotes a high level of uric acid, which may trigger gout or other rheumatic conditions.

General health and vitality

Nutritional imbalances and deficiencies

Signs of nutritional deficiencies are mainly concentrated in the nails, which are particularly sensitive to changes in the constituents and supply of blood. Sudden or acute nutritional deficiencies are usually denoted by a single mark on each nail. More chronic conditions may also affect the very shape and construction of the nail.

Because it is known that nails take on average six months to grow, any marking seen in the nail can be timed, which then gives a pretty clear indication of when the illness or incident took place.

Look for ...

1 Distortions, irregular growth, vertical or horizontal ridging, or nails that are either concave or convex, all point to nutritional deficiencies and mineral imbalances of some sort or other.
2 White specks in the nails suggest either a calcium or zinc imbalance.
3 Very soft nails, especially ones that seem to split or break easily.
4 Lines in the palm that run pale when the fingers are flexed back.
5 Broken skin-ridge patterns suggest long-term deficiencies, especially of vitamins.
6 Chains in the Life, Head and Heart lines may denote mineral imbalances.

Reading the main signs: nutritional imbalances

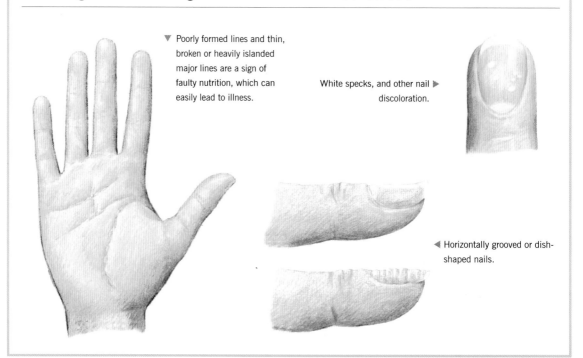

▼ Poorly formed lines and thin, broken or heavily islanded major lines are a sign of faulty nutrition, which can easily lead to illness.

White specks, and other nail ▶ discoloration.

◀ Horizontally grooved or dish-shaped nails.

Common symptoms and illnesses related to nutritional imbalances

Symptoms Lack of energy, headache, constipation, diarrhoea, vomiting, weight loss or gain, haemorrhoids, irritable bowel

Illnesses Coeliac disease, diverticular disease, rickets, diabetes, cancer, gall-bladder disease, night blindness, anaemia, arrested growth, insomnia

4 When the thumb is pressed against the edge of the palm, on the back of the hand, if the muscle at the base of the V-shaped join between thumb and palm is firm and springy when it humps up, then vitality and recuperative powers are good. If this muscle is flaccid, or produces a depression rather than a hump, the constitution is at a low ebb.

Taking action:

- Ginseng to boost strength and vitality; herbal tonics such as schisandra, pollen, sage and ginger.

Taking action

It is said that serious nutritional deficiencies are unlikely to occur in the West, where most people can afford to eat a balanced diet. Yet deformities and markings in the nails are commonly seen by the average hand analyst, which suggests that nutritional deficiencies are rife. It seems that bad eating habits, lack of time and modern food production methods are robbing us of nutrients, and so many of us turn to vitamin and mineral supplementation.

Because of their interrelated action, vitamins and minerals should not be taken in isolation, as too much of one can seriously deplete another. A multivitamin and mineral tablet is perhaps the safest way to boost nutrition when necessary (remembering not to exceed the stated dose), while making sure that you are definitely getting a good all-round diet.

Vitality

Look for ...

1 Well-padded and springy mounts.
2 A well-constructed and well-endowed base to the palm (the mounts of Venus and Luna).
3 Good, strong, clearly marked lines, especially the Life line.

Reading the main signs: general vitality

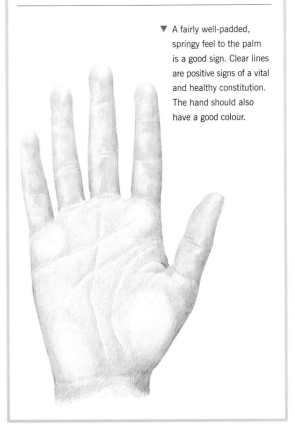

▼ A fairly well-padded, springy feel to the palm is a good sign. Clear lines are positive signs of a vital and healthy constitution. The hand should also have a good colour.

Reflexology for hands

Reflexology is based on the theory that the muscles and organs inside our bodies are linked to corresponding areas in our feet, hands and ears. The body is divided into ten areas, with a midpoint line running vertically down the centre. The five zones on the left side of your body find their reflex points in your left foot, hand and ear, while those on your right side have their corresponding connections in the right extremities.

Any upset at one end of the link produces an effect at the other end. The therapeutic method used in reflexology is massage. So, for example, massaging the area a little way below your fourth toe has a healing effect on your lungs and bronchial regions (see illustrations for correspondences). All the organs within a zone are interrelated, so a problem with one organ may mean that the others may be affected, too – and treating one will also affect the others.

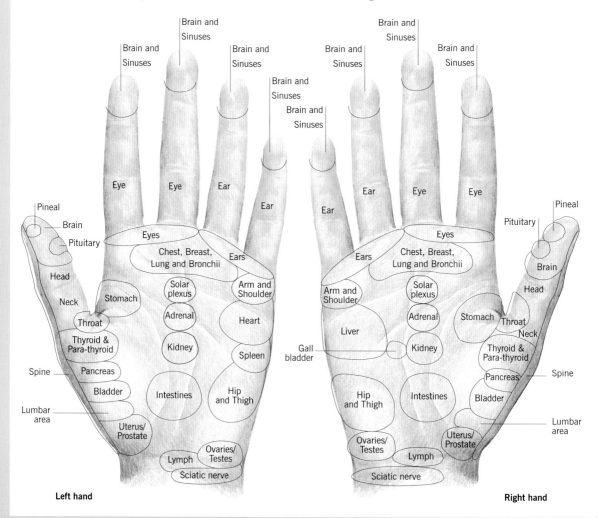

Left hand

Right hand

Massage techniques

Reflexology massage consists of applying direct, though not too firm, pressure with the side of your thumb tip, pressing down gently with a slow, circular motion. Any tingling sensation or sharp pain that is felt suggests a problem. Massaging a reflex point is said to stimulate the corresponding organ into eliminating toxins, restoring the system's chemical equilibrium, helping the organ to heal itself, and encouraging healing to take place throughout the body.

Reflexology and the hands

While reflexology usually concentrates on the feet, the hand is no less receptive – with the great advantage that we can treat ourselves any time, in any place, using the thumb of one hand to massage the other hand.

A little practice will soon show where to find the right spot, principally by virtue of its tenderness, and you may even experience a physical sensation when you hit the exact spot and start applying pressure. Some reflexologists maintain that they can locate a reflex point because it is often found sitting in a little depression, into which the thumb tip slips neatly as it slides over the skin.

Reflex points on the hand

Essential differences occur between right and left hands, depending on the location of an organ in your body. When muscles or organs come in pairs, each will correspond to the appropriate hand. When the organs are found down your central midline, they will be connected to both hands.

Common correspondences

Here are some common disorders that might benefit from reflexology. Give yourself a treatment when you feel discomfort, or do it as a daily routine to keep your body cleansed.

Stress and tension
Stress often tenses the abdominal muscles and so impedes relaxation. Massage the solar plexus reflexes in both hands.

Mental tiredness
Stimulate the brain reflexes on your thumb tips.

Respiratory problems
Stimulate the lung reflexes. Massage of both adrenal reflexes is especially helpful for asthma.

Digestive disorders
Massage the intestinal and/or liver reflexes in both hands.

Backache
Work variously on the spine, neck and sciatic nerve reflexes.

Poor memory
Stimulate the adrenal gland and brain reflexes.

Menstrual problems
Work on the pituitary gland, ovary and uterus reflexes. Pregnant women should seek advice first and always avoid reflexology on any reproductive organs.

The common cold
Apply pressure to reflexes for the lungs, bronchial area, sinuses, kidneys and adrenal glands.

Hypertension (high blood pressure)
This must obviously be treated by a doctor, but reflexology may help to stop it from developing in the first place. Work on the heart, the kidneys and adrenals, the thyroid, the para-thyroid and the liver.

Obesity
Encourage weight reduction by toning your digestive system and stimulating the efficient elimination of wastes, thereby discouraging fluid retention. Do this by applying pressure, for a few minutes each day, on the lymph gland reflexes, the intestinal area, and the kidney and liver reflexes.

Other conditions

Cancer

The signs listed below are thought by some to be associated with the disease (in general only, not to specific types), although there are countless exceptions and a great deal of research remains to be done:

Look for ...

1 Broken ridge lines.

2 A clear, well-formed island low down in the Life line.

3 Little yellowish, callus-like areas of skin on the Venus or Luna mounts, or running down the outside edge of the thumb towards the wrist.

Taking action

- Early detection and treatment give the best chances of combating the disease.
- Phytotherapy – a diet rich in fruit and vegetables – is believed to help prevent cancer.
- A theory that dairy products may help trigger testicular and breast cancer is under investigation at the current time.

Dental problems

Look for ...

These apply whether the problems are inherited, caused by poor diet or whatever.

1 Tiny, oblique lines just over the Heart line directly below the webbing between the ring and little fingers. (Not to be confused with the Medical Stigmata; see page 35.)

2 A ladder-like shape of little lines below the Heart line directly beneath the ring and little finger suggests a calcium deficiency, which could well affect the teeth and gums.

Taking action

- Calcium is essential for healthy teeth.
- Calc. Phos. and Calc. Fluor. are recommended for decay and for promoting good enamel. Combination R, comprising Calc. Fluor., Calc. Phos., Ferr. Phos., Mag. Phos. and Silica, is recommended for the formation of good teeth, in troublesome teething, to ease toothache and for other dental problems.

Fever

Look for ...

1 A full Apollo mount.

2 High fever often leaves a horizontal groove across all the nails.

Taking action ...

- Borage has a cooling action on fever, while eucalyptus may also help intermittent cases.
- Ferr. Phos. tissue salt.

Headaches and migraine

Look for ...

A tendency to headaches, particularly migraine, may be detected by tiny indentations in the Head line. Groups of these highlight periods when the attacks are more concentrated.

Taking action

- Calcium.
- Feverfew is now gaining recognition in orthodox medical circles as a potent cure for migraine.

Quick fixes

Rose quartz has a calming and soothing effect: place it on your forehead to help cool and ease the pain.

Common headache-related symptoms and illnesses

Symptoms Dizzy spells, flashing lights, nausea, vomiting, intolerance of bright light

Illnesses Severe stress, fever, allergies, depression, stroke, high blood pressure, kidney disease, tumour, anaemia, meningitis

- Combination F tissue salts – Kali. Phos., Mag. Phos., Nat. Mur. and Silica – for both headaches and migraine.
- Certain foodstuffs, especially coffee, chocolate and cheese, are known triggers of migraine attacks. Using a process of elimination may help you to find which of these (or other) foods is affecting you.

Reading the main signs: headaches and migraine

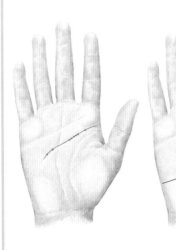

▲ Tiny pin-pricks punctuating the Head line are classic indicators of a susceptibility to migraine.

▲ An Allergy line also present may help to throw light on the cause of the condition.

- Many headaches are caused by tension in the neck and shoulders. Osteopathy and massage can bring relief to long-standing problems.

Herpes Simplex

A viral condition that is believed to be aggravated by stress.

Look for ...
Begins with some irritation in isolated spots on, or between, the fingers and sometimes on the palm. The affected skin reddens and little watery vesicles subsequently develop.

Surgery

Presence of a marking need not imply that surgery is inevitable, merely that there is a susceptibility to a condition that may necessitate surgical intervention.

Look for:
1 Certain conditions that may require an internal operation are sometimes denoted by a group of lines that form themselves into a diamond or triangle attached to the Life line about two-thirds of the way down the palm. This pattern is found in many hands and may relate to various disorders ranging from digestive problems involving the gall bladder, diseases of the female reproductive organs that may require a hysterectomy, hiatus hernia and urological disorders in men.
2 A clean break in the Life line. If one hand only shows the break, there may be mitigating protective markings that offset any need for surgery – a square over the break or a secondary inner line overlapping it, for example. If both hands show the same break at the same point in time, the chance of needing surgery becomes more likely.

Appendix of Complementary Therapies

Here are general outlines of the complementary therapies referred to in this book.

Acupressure

Acupressure is a Chinese method of healing that has been practised for over 3,000 years and which works on the 'meridians' – energy channels that run in a network through the body. In a healthy body, the *Ch'i*, or essential energy, flows freely and evenly through the meridians. But when blockages occur, the body becomes unbalanced, Ch'i is trapped and disease occurs. Throughout this network are located key pressure points that can be worked on to release blockages and restore the body to its natural balance. The practitioner massages these points, using only the thumbs, to either increase or decrease the flow of energy and thereby restore the body to health. (See also Acupuncture, below.)

Acupuncture

A similar therapy to acupressure but, instead of using the thumbs, the therapist inserts fine needles into the pressure points to rebalance the flow of Ch'i. In both acupuncture and acupressure, the meridians are believed to be linked to specific organs, and stimulation of the pressure points indirectly affects their corresponding organs. These methods of healing can greatly assist many conditions, including the pain of childbirth.

Aromatherapy

Cleopatra is said to have recognized the power of flower essences and used them to great effect in her beauty routines. The glorious essential oils of flowers and herbs, spices and resins have for millennia been distilled and used in both cosmetic and medicinal preparations to boost health and well-being. Whether massaged into the skin, inhaled, or added to the bath, aromatic oils have the power to affect both mind and body. Fragrant and beautiful though they may be, they are powerful stimulants and advice in their use should be sought – especially in certain conditions such as pregnancy or cancer.

Bach Flower Remedies

Originated by Dr Edward Bach at the beginning of the twentieth century, these remedies consist of 38 preparations that are potentized flower essences, with a 39th one called Recovery Remedy (formally known as Rescue Remedy). The Bach Flower Remedies are designed to rebalance negative emotions and put the individual back on the road to recovery.

Bates eye exercises

Working at the beginning of the twentieth century, Dr W.H. Bates was a pioneer of natural eye care who postulated many theories and exercises to explain and remedy eye problems – including the idea that most eye disorders were caused by poor nutrition, emotional strain and stress. Though vilified by his contemporaries, many of his practices were later vindicated and his eye exercises became widespread. For example, medical studies have shown that an adequate intake of the anti-oxidant vitamins A, C and E is an effective measure against developing cataracts. In addition, two trace elements, selenium and magnesium, have been found useful for cataracts – both in their prevention and as an adjunct to conventional treatment.

Breathing exercises for relaxation

Unfortunately, most of us simply don't breathe efficiently or effectively, breathing shallowly into the top of our chests instead of taking each breath down deeply to reach the lower parts of our lungs. Correct breathing can aid relaxation and even reduce high blood pressure. Breathing exercises, which are designed to teach us to breathe correctly, can help us not only stay calmer and more focused, but also improve our vitality and health.

Colour/light therapy

The Ancient Egyptians used colour as part of their healing therapies because they recognized that certain colours corresponded to particular organs and states of mind. Modern psychological studies have endorsed colour therapy as a healing tool and have established that colour has a definite affect on our moods. Red, for example, activates us physically, while green and blue have a soothing and calming effect.

Crystal therapy

Gemstones are believed to emit vibrations that can stimulate health and well-being. Each stone-type works on a different frequency, and so keys in to different conditions and states of mind. Rose quartz, for example, is said to soothe tension while Jade balances the emotions. Do you find you suddenly see gemstone pieces that strongly attract you? Or do you have gemstone jewellery that you would feel lost without? Well, it is said that a crystal finds you, not you it!

Exercise

Medical thinking now recognizes the benefits of exercise as an adjunct to good health. Getting moving and active can help in a range of conditions, not simply in reducing weight and keeping fit, but also to offset such conditions as osteoporosis, heart disease and cancer.

Herbalism

Herbal cures are a precursor to our modern medicines and, in fact, a good deal of the drugs we use today originate from plant extracts that have been used for thousands of years in the treatment of disease. Aspirin and quinine, for example, come from the bark of a tree.

Homeopathy

Although the principles of treating 'like with like' were recognized by the Ancient Greeks, our modern system of homeopathy was devised by Dr Samuel Hahnemann, a German physician who lived and worked in the nineteenth century. The therapy is based on remedies derived from natural substances that are believed to help the body cure itself by matching the medicine to the symptoms. Homeopathy is a holistic form of treatment that treats the individual, not the illness. (See also pages 126–7.)

Massage

From effleurage to reflexology, and petrissage to Reiki, the physically and mentally therapeutic effects of touch have been recognized for thousands of years. A diverse variety of maladies ranging from tension in the neck to severe sporting injuries can be treated with an appropriate form of massage and manipulation. (See also pages 114–15.)

Meditation

Not so much a therapy as a way of life, meditation takes time and practice to perfect but soon begins to repay every effort. The technique involves freeing the mind from thoughts, paying attention to one's breathing and entering a state of deep contemplation. Studies have shown that, because meditation calms the mind

so profoundly, it is an effective method of reducing such conditions as anxiety, insomnia and high blood pressure.

Nutritional supplements

There are somewhere in the region of thirteen major vitamins and twenty-five essential minerals that are required by the body in order for it to function at its best. Ideally, a balanced diet should be able to supply all our nutritional needs, but modern processing of our foodstuffs strips much of the goodness away. Though long refuted by the medical profession, the need to supplement our diets under certain circumstances with an additional dose of multivitamins and minerals is at last being recognized by many doctors. However, excessive quantities of some vitamins and minerals can be as damaging as too few, so sticking to the recommended daily allowance is advisable, as is seeking medical advice.

Reflexology

A form of massage that works along similar principles to acupressure, reflexology is another holistic therapy that stimulates pressure points to release blockages in the body's organs that are believed to be responsible for causing disease. Typically, reflexology works on the soles of the feet, but it is also perfect for the hands. Specific areas on the hands/feet correspond to a particular organ or part of the body. The art of reflexology has been practised in the East for thousands of years and was introduced into the West in the early 1900s by an American doctor, William Fitzgerald. No scientific explanation has yet been found to satisfactorily explain how or why it works – that it does work, however, many people would say is indisputable. (See also pages 136–7.)

Shiatsu

Working on similar principles to acupressure, shiatsu is a Japanese form of massage that also rebalances the body by stimulating pressure points along the meridians. The name means 'finger pressure', although the hands, elbows, knees and even feet may be used to apply the force necessary to loosen and relax the patient in order to stimulate the flow of Ch'i, or life force, through the body.

Tissue salt therapy

Also known as Biochemic remedies, this homeopathic form of therapy was developed by Dr Wilhelm Schuessler in the late nineteenth century. The system consists of twelve tissue salts that, it is claimed, the body needs to achieve homeostasis, or perfect balance, in order to maintain its health and well-being. An example of one in the range is Nat. Sulph. (sodium sulphate), said to be useful in helping to relieve morning sickness.

Yoga

Long practised in the East, yoga is a type of exercise that incorporates posture, breathing and meditation techniques to balance the mind, body and spirit. There are many forms, such as Ashtanga and Raja, but perhaps the best known in the West is Hatha yoga, which combines 'asanas' (steady, held poses), movements and posture with 'pranayama', or controlled breathing. Yoga has many benefits, not least of which is that it leads to a state of deep relaxation. But yoga can do more. It can improve fitness and suppleness, fight fatigue and help to relieve digestive disorders and many other ailments besides. However, the ultimate aim in practising yoga is to achieve spiritual awareness and enlightenment.

Index

Further Reading

The Complete Illustrated Guide to Palmistry, Peter West.
Shaftesbury: Element Books, 1998

The Hand of Man, Noel Jaquin.
London: Faber & Faber, 1933

Hand Psychology, Andrew Fitzherbert.
New York: Avery, 1989

Life Lines, Peter West.
Berkshire: Quantum, 1998

Living Palmistry, Sasha Fenton and Malcolm Wright.
London: Aquarian Press, 1990

Palmistry 4 Today, Frank C. Clifford.
London: Rider, 2002

Practical Palmistry, David Brandon-Jones.
London: Rider, 1981

Your Life in Your Hands, Beryl Hutchinson.
Saffron Walden: Neville Spearman, 1967

Other books on palmistry by Lori Reid

The Art of Hand Reading
London: Dorling Kindersley, 1996

The Elements of Handreading
Shaftesbury: Element Books, 1994

Palmistry in the 21st Century
London: Piatkus, 2000

Acknowledgements

EDDISON•SADD EDITIONS

Commissioning Editor Liz Wheeler
Project Editors Ann Kay, Tessa Monina
Editor Mary Lambert
Proofreader Nikky Twyman
Indexer Dorothy Frame
Production Karyn Claridge and Charles James

Art Director Elaine Partington
Senior Art Editor Hayley Cove
Designers Axis Design
Mac Designer Brazzle Atkins
Illustrations Amy Burch
Line illustrations Paul Beebee